300754044R

D0120260

The Critical Idiom

Founder Editor: JOHN D. JUMP (1969–1976)

17 *The Epic*

The Epic / *Paul Merchant*

Methuen

LONDON and NEW YORK

for RAMONA

41344

3007540LLR

First published 1971
by Methuen & Co. Ltd
11 New Fetter Lane, London EC4P 4EE
Reprinted twice
Reprinted 1984

Published in the USA by
Methuen & Co.
in association with Methuen, Inc.
733 Third Avenue, New York, NY 10017

© *Paul Merchant*

Printed in Great Britain
by J. W. Arrowsmith Ltd, Bristol

ISBN 0 416 19700 0

Contents

Founder Editor's Preface

The volumes composing the Critical Idiom deal with a wide variety of key terms in our critical vocabulary. The purpose of the series differs from that served by the standard glossaries of literary terms. Many terms are adequately defined for the needs of students by the brief entries in these glossaries, and such terms do not call for attention in the present series. But there are other terms which cannot be made familiar by means of compact definitions. Students need to grow accustomed to them through simple and straightforward but reasonably full discussions. The main purpose of this series is to provide such discussions.

Many critics have borrowed methods and criteria from currently influential bodies of knowledge or belief that have developed without particular reference to literature. In our own century, some of them have drawn on art-history, psychology, or sociology. Others, strong in a comprehensive faith, have looked at literature and literary criticism from a Marxist or a Christian or some other sharply defined point of view. The result has been the importation into literary criticism of terms from the vocabularies of these sciences and creeds. Discussions of such bodies of knowledge and belief in their bearing upon literature and literary criticism form a natural extension of the initial aim of the Critical Idiom.

Because of their diversity of subject-matter, the studies in the series vary considerably in structure. But all authors have tried to give as full illustrative quotation as possible, to make reference whenever appropriate to more than one literature, and to write in such a way as to guide readers towards the short bibliographies in which they have made suggestions for further reading.

John D. Jump

University of Manchester

Prefatory Note

The term 'epic' can be defined in two very different ways, either narrowly, through a study of a select group of classical epics, or more broadly, by taking into consideration the whole range of writing which might be called epic. The former definition would confine the term 'epic' to long narrative poems, written in hexameters or their equivalent, concentrating either on a hero (Achilles, Beowulf) or on a civilization, like Rome or Christendom. These two types might be distinguished by the terms 'primary' (or 'oral' or 'primitive') and 'secondary' or 'literary'. In the first group Homer's *Iliad* and *Odyssey* would be joined by *Beowulf* and perhaps the *Song of Roland*. The second group, dominated by Vergil's *Aeneid*, would include a series of poems modelled to some extent upon Homer and Vergil, and each contributing something to the tradition – Lucan's *Pharsalia*, Tasso's *Gerusalemme Liberata*, Milton's *Paradise Lost*. F. L. Lucas, in his entry 'Epic' in Chambers' *Encyclopaedia*, offers a useful summary of the 'essential epic qualities':

> Unity of action, rapidity, the art of beginning in the middle; the use of the supernatural, of prophecy, of the underworld; the ornamental simile, the recurrent epithet; and above all, a nobility truthful, unstrained, incomparable except at moments in the sagas of the north.

Outside this closely defined category lie a far larger number of works having a close, sometimes direct, relation to the conventional epics, and this book concerns itself with this broad tradition also. One of the greatest strengths of the epic tradition is its variety, and a study which confined itself to the long narrative poems, superlative though they are, would do epic an injustice.

I have chosen to discuss the term 'epic' through a series of brief critical studies of individual works, in the belief that the lines of the tradition can best be seen through comparison and illustration, however brief. The conclusion, that the epic is a still developing and expanding form, may be at first sight surprising, but the wealth of overtly 'epic' writing in at least three fields during this century threatened to make the final chapter the longest of the four.

I am most grateful to Terence McCarthy for his translations from *Beowulf* which are used in the first chapter. All other translations, except where acknowledged in the text, are my own. I would like to thank Professor Jump in particular for his kindness and invaluable editorial advice; I have also been very much helped by my parents, by Lynne Browne, Derek Longhurst, Hazel and Arthur Jarvis, and my wife, to whom the book is dedicated.

I

Introduction

There would be no value in attempting a simple definition of a literary form which includes the *Iliad*, *The Prelude* and *War and Peace*. One may profitably, however, ask what it is that these and other epics have in common. In an article reporting from North Vietnam in the *Sunday Times* for 21 July 1968, Mary McCarthy described the war in these terms:

> ... their defence of their lan d has the quality of an epic, i.e., of a work of art surpassing the dimensions of realism.

Ezra Pound, in his *ABC of Reading* (London, 1961, p. 46) offers another apparently simple definition:

> An epic is a poem including history.

These two phrases, 'surpassing the dimensions of realism' and 'including history', represent the two poles within which we place the experience described as 'epic'. In *War and Peace*, for instance, history is included in the work of art, in the sense that the echoes aroused in the reader's imagination refer to events both before and after the creation of the work; but this is not to say that history is in any sense the subject of the work.

The double relation of epic, to history on the one hand and to everyday reality on the other, emphasizes clearly two of its most important original functions. It was a chronicle, a 'book of the tribe', a vital record of custom and tradition, and at the same time a story-book for general entertainment. The latter aspect of epic, its value simply as a story, needs no elaboration; but epic itself may have originated in the need for an established history. In A.D. 98 Tacitus noted at the opening of his study of Germany (*Germania* c.2) that the Germanic tribes of his day celebrate the founders of their race in 'ancient songs, the only kind of folk-memory or chronicle available to them'. This function of epic is seen vividly in action in a famous passage in *Odyssey* 8, where the Phaeacian bard Demodocus sings, at the request of Odysseus in disguise, the story of the Trojan Horse, an episode in which Odysseus himself played a prominent part. The hero is so moved by the recitation that he weeps, and so reveals his identity. The apparent speed with which the tale had already established itself in the bard's repertoire can be paralleled by a similar moment in the first book of Vergil's *Aeneid*. Aeneas and his men are confronted in Carthage with the walls of the newly built temple, which have upon them scenes from the siege of Troy. One presumes that neither Homer nor Vergil would have suggested that it was likely in literal terms for a man's fame to precede him so rapidly, but the point is surely being made that for the great hero the events of his own lifetime have already become subjects for epic.

The sophisticated relationship of the poet to his material, his awareness of historical perspective, reminds us that even our earliest epics date from a period when epic narrative had already been in use for some hundreds of years. We have no examples of the first lays; we can only make deductions from the poems we have inherited; and in these, two pressures are already in operation – the pressure on the one hand of a poet's imagination and artistry, and on the other of an audience's desire for entertainment. The poems are no longer purely chronicles, they are already to some extent fictional.

In the Old English *Beowulf* there is a similar awareness of historical perspective on the part of the poet, which in this case takes the form of a nostalgia for the glories of the past. Two passages spoken by the Danish king Hrothgar illustrate this

attitude clearly. In the first, Hrothgar is offering the hero gifts after
he has mortally wounded the monster Grendel:

> Many times I have given a reward for less
> to an inferior man, to a feebler warrior,
> and honoured him with gifts. You, by your deeds,
> have secured for yourself an endless renown.
>
> (ll. 951–5)

Eight hundred lines later, after Beowulf's underwater victory over
Grendel's mother, Hrothgar's speech of congratulation reaches its
climax in this passage:

> Have nothing to do with pride,
> noble warrior. Now the glory of your strength
> is for a moment. Sickness or the sword will come at once
> and rob you of your might –
> or the grip of fire, or the welling of the waves,
> or the onslaught of the sword, or the spear's flight,
> or terrible old age, or else the brightness of the eyes
> will fail and darken. O warrior,
> in a moment death will overpower you.
>
> (ll. 1760B–8)

It is this prevailing tone which leads J. R. R. Tolkien to state
in his famous essay '*Beowulf*: The Monsters and the Critics'
that:

> *Beowulf* is not an 'epic', not even a magnified 'lay'. No terms borrowed
> from Greek or other literatures exactly fit: there is no reason why they
> should. Though if we must have a term, we should choose rather
> 'elegy'.

The poet, in short, is using historical material for his own ends.
For Homer the background of his *Iliad* is the fall of a great
civilization; for the poet of *Beowulf* it is the passing of the old
heroes, the theme so simply introduced in the opening lines of the
poem:

> Yes, we have heard the greatness
> of the Danish kings in old days,
> how the heroes did courageous deeds.
>
> (ll. 1–3

In the last analysis, however, as Horace comments, the epic poem centres upon men; exceptional men, but none the less human:

> Many heroes lived before Agamemnon
> but all of them, unknown, unmourned,
> have slipped into dark oblivion
> because no poet praised them.
>
> (Odes IV, 9, 25–8

The epic hero's fame is directly linked with that of his bard; but the bard's quality depends no less on an ability to concentrate all his energies on his subject. It is this sharp focus on to the central figure in his massive isolation that gives the great epics their grandeur and universality. We are confronted not by a man at a moment in history, but by Man in History. We are all involved in what becomes of him.

Finally, there is one quality inherent in our use of the word 'epic' that should be discussed. It is implicit whenever we speak of an 'epic journey' or an 'epic struggle'; in the cinema we are familiar with the terms 'Biblical epic' and 'Epic Western'; Mary McCarthy and Ezra Pound use the words 'surpassing' and 'including'. In their different ways these usages all point to an underlying conception characteristic of epic – the notion of 'scale', 'mass', 'weight'. While the epic need not necessarily be long (and many are), it must be large in scale, it must have 'epic proportions'. In the chapters that follow, a number of such works will be examined, ranging from Homer to Ezra Pound, from the earliest epic to an epic still in progress, in an attempt to uncover the creative pattern underlying these expansive and ambitious 'poems including history'.

2
Classical Epic

We are surprisingly well informed about certain aspects of early
epic, and in particular about the manner of recitation. Homer's
account of the singing of the Phaeacian poet Demodocus in
Odyssey 8 has already been discussed to show the relationship of
the bard to his material. This superbly written book also offers
valuable evidence for the actual conditions of performance.

> A herald soon came bringing the famous singer,
> whom the Muse had befriended, giving good with evil:
> she had taken his eyes, but left him the gift of sweet song.
> Pontonous placed a silver chair among the banqueters,
> close to the stout pillar, and there
> he hung from a nail the melodious lyre,
> just there, above his head, guiding his hand
> to where it was.
>
> (8, 62–9)

The singer is blind. Perhaps we should not be too certain about
the poetic meaning of this celebrated image. The blindness may
symbolize the poetic use of imagination and memory, so important
to an oral poet; or it may reflect on a sociological circumstance,
that the blind man is at an advantage in the difficult task of im-
promptu composition. It may be even more simple, that the poet is
describing (and how vividly he does so, with the telling image of
the hand led to the lyre) an actual blind bard. Whichever expla-
nation we might prefer, one impression is inescapable – that of the
almost religious awe with which the poet describes one of his

fellow practitioners. In Book 22 Phemius, the bard in Odysseus's palace in Ithaca, claims immunity from the sentence passed on the suitors:

> You will regret it afterwards if you kill
> a bard, the singer for gods and men.
> I am self-taught, and God planted in my heart
> the various ways of song.

(22, 345–8)

Homer appears to be insisting on some theory of poetic inspiration, but at the same time the striking word 'self-taught' appears to imply a high degree of consciousness of technique in the poets.

To return to Book 8, the first lay sung by Demodocus concerns the quarrel between Odysseus and Achilles. This so moves Odysseus that King Alcinous suggests adjourning for an athletic contest. After the athletics the bard sings a story of the adultery of Aphrodite with Ares and the revenge of her husband Hephaestus. Later in the evening he sings a further tale, the story of the Wooden Horse:

> Prompted by God, he began and fashioned his song
> starting at the point where some of the Greeks sailed away
> in their well-benched boats, after burning their huts,
> while the others, together with famous Odysseus,
> lay hidden inside the horse in the main square of Troy.

(8, 499–503)

In the first of these recitations, the quarrel between Odysseus and Achilles, there can be seen the germ of a whole epic like the *Iliad*, which begins with a similar quarrel. It is easy to see how a story of this kind might be used for a brief lay, for a *chanson de geste*, or might develop into a full-length epic. The central theme of an epic need not be more complex than this. The second of the two stories, which was accompanied by a dance, perhaps a mime of the action, is of a different order. The writing is lighter and more humorous, the subject mythical rather than heroic. If the first relates to the *Iliad*, the second, more folk-tale than saga, seems closer to the *Odyssey*.

The third recitation, however, moves into the shadowy area behind the Homeric poems. Proclus, an early commentator on Homer, pointed out that the *Sack of Troy*, a poem in the Homeric cycle, began at this moment, with the Greeks sailing away, leaving the Wooden Horse behind. The phrase 'Starting at the point where...' echoes line 10 of the *Odyssey* itself, where the poet asks the Muse to help him to begin 'at some point or other'. Clearly the poets held in their heads a vast number of plots and synopses belonging to various points in the epic cycle, any one of which they would be prepared to relate in words of their own choosing. The *Iliad* ends before the Sack of Troy; the *Odyssey* begins after it. Is it possible that the poet deliberately inserted the Fall of Troy here in miniature, as an acknowledgement of the great theme which haunts the whole Trojan Cycle? If the effect is not as calculated as this might suggest, it is clear that the *Odyssey* poet regarded the connection of Odysseus with the Trojan Horse as an important piece of background information. In Book 4 (266–89) the same topic is raised when Menelaus describes the experience of being with Odysseus inside the Wooden Horse.

A short passage in *Beowulf* provides a remarkable parallel to the Homeric picture of a bard at work:

> At times one of the king's thanes,
> a proud man with a store of songs,
> who remembered a great many old traditions,
> composed a new tale, putting it together truthfully.
> In turn the man began cleverly to tell
> of Beowulf's journey, artfully reciting that apt story
> with skilful repetitions. He told everything
> he had heard said of Sigemund's deeds of valour,
> and many unknown things.
>
> (ll. 867B–76)

We are in the same world as Odysseus hearing his own name in an epic, and Aeneas seeing himself on the temple wall at Carthage. Here, however, the mechanism is not concealed or ignored, as it is in Homer and Vergil; we actually see the device used by the poet to suit his epic to the needs of the moment. Beowulf's deeds of valour are compared (artfully, as the poet reminds us) with the similar exploits of Sigemund. The substructure of the story is the old lay of Sigemund, both the familiar episodes and new ones, invented or now used for the first time. Into this framework the poet inserts the adventures of Beowulf, making out of the mixture a 'new tale'. Now if this composite tale is successful, he will repeat it, even when Beowulf is not there to be flattered. Eventually it is possible that the new tale will oust the old, and what was originally the lay of Sigemund will become a *Beowulf*.

This tendency of the successful to oust the less successful is even more true of the 'skilful repetitions', otherwise known as formulae. It has been shown (by Milman Parry and A. B. Lord, studying oral poets still composing in Yugoslavia, followed by Francis P. Magoun and Robert P. Creed in the field of *Beowulf*) that oral poets use their basic stock-in-trade, the formula, with great economy. Since the Homeric hexameter and the Anglo-Saxon alliterative measure impose great strains upon a poet, whenever he finds a phrase that both fits his metrical scheme and is pleasing in itself he will remember it and use it again. In time this will become formulaic, and will hold its own against phrases of the same metrical shape and similar meaning, unless other newer phrases are found to be more successful poetically, in which case the formulaic phrases will quickly be discarded in their favour. The result is a vast collection of specialized phrases, each designed exclusively for a particular place in the line, which the singer will use as his basic material. These phrases may remain unchallenged for centuries. The parting of Hector and Andromache in *Iliad* 6, one of the high moments of the poem, is almost three-quarters composed of inherited material. The first twenty-one lines of the *Odyssey* contain forty-five formulaic phrases. In the first twenty-five lines of *Beowulf* there are thirty-five word-groupings used elsewhere in Old English literature. Clearly this makes it impossible to talk of 'originality' in an oral poet, and the identity of the creator is at best blurred.

In using the words 'Homer' and 'poet' one is therefore begging any number of questions. But there are at the same time many features of both the *Iliad* and the *Odyssey* (symmetry, organization and other largely technical matters) which suggest the presence of an individual intellect in some relation to each of the poems. Whether we are faced with two such intellects, and what proportions of the poems as we have them can be called theirs, these are matters which may never be resolved completely. Perhaps the poems are the more compelling for that uncertainty.

HOMER AND THE OLD TESTAMENT

European literature begins with the Homeric epics. They are likely to have been the first works of art written down in Europe. In the Near East the Sumerian *Gilgamesh* and the Hebrew myths of Creation, Fall and Deluge stand in a similar relation to their literatures. There are certain features in all these works which arise from almost identical causes. In each case the writers look back to a period of extraordinary significance in an attempt to define in some way the nature of man and his relation to the world.

The Old Testament begins with the stories of the Creation and the Flood, and soon passes to the story of Abraham. There is a distinction to be made between the early myths, which are extremely similar to the Babylonian Creation and Flood myths, and may have been brought from Mesopotamia by Abraham and his people, and the story beginning with Abraham, which is not myth but history.

B

The mythological chapters, *Genesis* I–XI, 9, resemble the Babylonian and Sumerian versions in many respects; the Tree of Knowledge is first found in Babylonian mythology; the Biblical accounts of the Flood are uncannily similar to the account found in *Gilgamesh*. But whereas the *Gilgamesh* story is a single version, the early chapters of *Genesis* clearly provide two accounts. The first (to be seen for instance in chapters I and V) has a large number of repeated phrases ('Let there be . . . and there was . . . after its/their kind . . . be fruitful and multiply . . . these are the generations of . . .') and a monotheistic view of God. The other account (chapters II–IV) has a more fluid and varied style, with greater human interest, and the God is anthropomorphic, He breathes into man's nostrils, He plants the garden, He walks in the garden. Clearly the two sources have been combined. This is even more striking in the Flood narrative, where the two sources are used alternately. The separation of these different sources was undertaken during the last century, in an activity known as the Higher Criticism, a technique allied to the methods described in the previous section for dealing with the Homeric sources. In both cases critics came to similar conclusions; the works were seen to have been composed at the end of a long tradition, during which the material had been handed down for some hundreds of years before reaching its final form. The discrepancies between the parts of the narrative provided much of the evidence required to unravel some of these secrets of authorship.

Despite this close similarity between the early books of the Old Testament, *Gilgamesh* and Homer, there still remains an essential difference. *Gilgamesh* is the story of a man's quest for glory and immortality. The Homeric epics have at their core the heroes Achilles and Odysseus respectively. The Old Testament has as its theme the special relationship between God and His chosen people. In the last analysis, however much the work may depend upon the methods and techniques of epic, the dactic quality of the Biblical narrative sets it apart from other epics.

This difference has been superbly illustrated by Erich Auerbach in the first chapter of his book *Mimesis*. Analysing Homer's account of the scar of Odysseus in *Odyssey* 19, he compares the treatment of the sacrifice of Isaac in *Genesis* XXII. For Homer the details of the story are everything – he is even prepared to leave the reader in suspense for more than seventy lines at one of the poem's greatest moments of crisis, simply so as to describe the circumstances in which Odysseus received his scar. For the Biblical writer the details are of little importance – the dealings of God with Abraham take place against a shadowy background stretching deep into the past, which is never discussed. The Biblical story has claims to universal authority; the Homeric tale concerns us as individuals.

Another comparison between the Bible and Homer offers a similar illustration. In the Old Testament the element of repetition, the repeated phrases and frequent genealogies, gives an impression of the importance of ritual and the necessity for the preservation of religious custom and tradition. In Homer the repetitions and informative digressions seem more a part of the story-teller's art; the pleasure is in the telling, not in the message conveyed by the tale.

It is sometimes difficult to appreciate the ability of an oral culture to create sustained works of art; this is made possible chiefly by its capacity for memory. An article, 'Gipsies', by John Seymour in the *Listener*, 6 February 1969, shows this clearly:

The Gipsies are repositories of folk-memory. Just as in Hungary they retained the Magyar folk-music when it had died out among the settled people, so in Britain they preserve the folk-lore, folk-song and music lost among the literate population. They have an oral culture and the most astonishing memories. If a Gipsy sings a song once, from an Elizabethan folk-song to the latest pop song, the chances are that he will remember every word of it.

Relying on a similar memory, the singers of the Homeric poems
produce works that compare extremely favourably with the literary
compositions of later generations.

An example of Homeric composition at its best may be seen in
the close of Book 5 of the *Odyssey*. Odysseus has been adrift for
two days and nights in the sea after the wreck of the raft in which
he sailed from Calypso's island. In the first of three similes the
moment is described when Odysseus sights the land of Phaeacia:

> Then he just caught sight of land
> looking ahead sharply, lifted on a great wave.
> And just as a father's life is a blessed thing
> to his children – he lies in the harsh grip of disease,
> wasting away for ever as an evil spirit assaults him,
> but the gods have freed the lucky man from his pain –
> so the land with its trees was a blessing to Odysseus
> and he swam, straining to set foot on the shore.

$$(5, 392-9)$$

Immediately obvious is the economy with which the essential
elements are illustrated – the length of time, the pain, the relief
of bad fortune turning to good, we note the key words, 'blessed',
'lucky', 'blessing' (all from the same root in Greek). This economy,
however, would be true of any good story-teller. What makes the
Homeric poems outstanding is the accuracy and brevity with which
they illustrate the *inessential* elements. In the second line, for
instance,

> looking ahead sharply, lifted on a great wave,

we are given both a visual picture of Odysseus's face, with the
eyes straining to the shore, and an incidental reference to the
violence of the sea. The adverb 'sharply', also, not only describes
the type of look, but at the same time refers subtly and obliquely
to the character of Odysseus, a character already established by a
number of delicate touches of the same kind. In the simile itself
the comparison between the father returning to health and

Odysseus reaching land gains in value when applied to the story as a whole. Where the poet digresses to describe the man's illness, the details set up echoes and association which enrich the story. The mention of the children, for instance, reminds us of the relationship between Odysseus and Telemachus which is so important to the epic; and the antithesis between the 'evil spirit' and the 'gods' offers a kind of parallel to the conflict between Poseidon and Athena with which the *Odyssey* begins.

Thirty lines later another significant moment is marked by a simile:

> Then a great wave took him on the rough coast
> where his skin would have been flayed, his bones broken,
> but Pallas Athena put this plan in his head:
> he gripped the rock with both hands and held on,
> and hung there groaning as the great wave passed over.
> But when he was done with that, the undertow
> caught him again and flung him far out to sea.
> And just as a cuttlefish is dragged from its lair
> with scores of pebbles sticking to its suckers,
> so the skin was flayed from his strong hands
> and stuck to the rock. And the great wave covered him.
>
> (5, 425–35)

The comparison here is simpler, and the interest in the simile for its own sake perhaps less extensive; but once again the clarity and vividness of the picture is characteristic of the best of Homer. Just as in the earlier moment, where the 'great wave' offered a sight of land, so again, economically, a 'great wave' is responsible for the new turn of events. Again, the intelligence of Odysseus is commented upon (more specifically this time, in Athena's patronage) and we learn incidentally also of his strength, in the penultimate line. The simile itself is famous. The choice of subject reveals a fundamental feature of the civilization which produced the poem, its complete familiarity with the sea and its instinctive knowledge of that element as the most important single influence on its art.

In the two lines of the simile itself, there is a more important feature. At first sight the homeliness of the subject seems naïve and unsophisticated, but the simplicity is an indication not of *naïveté* but of an affinity with natural objects which is one of the secrets of Greek art. It is here that the distinction between Greek and Biblical epic is most pronounced. By comparison with the purpose-ful epic of the Hebrews, the Homeric poems seem to take an almost idolatrous pleasure simply in observing the world about them. Protagoras was in the mainstream of Greek thought when he observed that 'Man is the measure of all things.' In Homer the gods behave like humans; except that his humans are more adult.

The last lines of this fifth book of the *Odyssey* are marked by one more simile, as Odysseus reaches land and falls asleep. While the Greeks were familiar with the sea, they also feared it, and the peaceful close of the book expresses perfectly the mariner's relief at touching dry land. Odysseus sees a pair of olive trees, one wild, one cultivated, and beneath them a heap of fallen leaves:

> Seeing this, godlike hardy Odysseus was glad
> and lay right down, heaping up a pile of leaves.
> In the same way as a man puts a brand into black ashes
> in the distant fields where there are no neighbours,
> saving a spark of fire, no need to search elsewhere,
> so Odysseus covered himself in leaves. And Athena
> poured sleep on his eyes, to bring a quick end
> to his hard labours, and she covered his dear eyelids.
>
> (5, 486–end)

Again the technique is simple without being naïve – the connecting idea in the words 'covering', 'heaping', 'pouring' – but once again the poetry is quite strikingly successful at evoking in a few words the close relationship between man and the world around him. It is this close concentration on the single man in his environ-ment that epic is so well qualified to undertake.

As we read the *Odyssey* as a whole, we see it as a superb combination of folk-tale, sailors' yarn and remembered history. We become involved in the excitement of the story – the voyages of Odysseus, the maturing of Telemachus, the wooing of Penelope and the final vengeance on the Suitors – but it is at moments like the peaceful close of Book 5 that we understand what makes the whole work possible.

As a story alone it would be hard to improve on it; but even its narrative qualities are overshadowed by the charm and precision of its descriptions. The poet of the *Iliad* and *Odyssey* can hardly have been blind from birth.

HEROIC EPIC: ILIAD AND BEOWULF

The *Odyssey* is essentially a tale of adventure. The main characters, Odysseus, Penelope, Telemachus, are each placed in the classic situations for such a tale – the hero wandering and returning home, the wife surrounded by suitors, the son searching for his father. These situations themselves are developed as one would expect. The wandering hero meets a witch and a giant, loses his companions, visits the Underworld, finds Fairyland in Phaeacia; the wife weaves a web and unravels it to deceive her suitors; the son stands by his father in the final battle. The story is told with a keen delight in the changes of mood and texture, in a sophisticated style. Behind the fairy-tale, however, the Fall of Troy broods in the background, the great myth of the end of a civilization which formed a focus for the heroic lays being sung during the growth of the Homeric poems. In the *Iliad* these lays came together to form a masterpiece quite different from the *Odyssey*. In chapter 9 of the treatise *On the Sublime*, traditionally attributed to Longinus, the author assigns the *Odyssey* to the old age of Homer, who appreciated the vigour of war in his prime, then turned to the fabulous world of fairy-tale in his age. If the *Odyssey* is in some senses the ancestor of the novel, the *Iliad* is certainly the greatest in a line of heroic poetry which also, among early epics, includes *Beowulf* and the *Song of Roland*.

The theme of the *Iliad* is the anger of one man, Achilles; its background is the Fall of Troy; its context is war. In *Beowulf* the reign of one man, the good king Beowulf, is the theme, the background is the close of a civilization, and the context heroic. Similarly in the *Song of Roland* the chivalry of Roland is set against the wars between the Franks and the Saracens, and again the context is war and heroism. The relationship of the *Iliad* to its hero, however, puts it in a different class from the other two epics. In those works Beowulf and Roland are the heroes of their respective sagas, and so stand at the centre of the poems. Achilles is not in that sense the hero of a saga; he is not the only outstanding Greek. But his anger (the first word in the poem) is a unique event and it is around this, an unlikely theme for an epic, that the poem grew.

Achilles does not participate in the action for the first two thirds of the *Iliad*. In Book 18, after the death of Patroclus, Achilles enters to set off a chain of events which end in the death of Hector and the funeral of Patroclus. In the early books, however, he is noticeable for his absence, which is explained by the quarrel in the First Book. At the end of the first third of the epic, in Book 9, when the Trojan fortunes are at their height, Achilles is approached for help; but after this moment of tension the initiative returns to Hector for the middle third of the epic. There has been some discussion by critics as to how a hero absent for so long, and preoccupied with such a trivial irritation, is able not only to hold the stage, but even to compel our attention so effectively. To answer the question one must again return to the concept of scale. We are interested in the anger of Achilles not as anger, nor as the anger of this man, but as an anger so massive that thousands of men on both sides must die to satisfy it. Shakespeare shows great understanding of this fact in his *Troilus and Cressida*. Achilles in that play has een called a 'spoilt child'; but if so, it is a child of epic proportions, who is capable of greeting Hector with the play's most ambitious peech:

> Tell me, you heavens, in which part of his body
> Shall I destroy him, whether there, or there, or there?
> That I may give the local wound a name,
> And make distinct the very breach whereat
> Hector's great spirit flew. Answer me, heavens!
>
> (V, 5, 241 ff.)

When Achilles is not the centre of interest the poet allows most of the heroes to hold the stage for long periods – on the Greek side Menelaus (Book 3), Diomedes (Book 5), Ajax (Book 7), Patroclus (Book 17) and on the Trojan side Paris and in particular Hector, whose parting from Andromache in Book 6 is possibly the best-known episode in the poem. Characteristic also of this poem, as of the *Odyssey*, is its attention to detail. In Book 11 old Nestor, the 'good old chronicle' of Shakespeare's play, describes – in over a hundred lines – an episode from his youth, a cattle raid against the Elians, in which he captured 'fifty herds of cattle, as many flocks of sheep, of swine, spreading herds of goats, a hundred and fifty chestnut horses, all mares, many of them with foals'. Leaving aside the tempting speculation that the Trojan War itself may have begun as a similar raid, one cannot help noticing throughout Nestor's account the cleverness with which the garrulous old man is characterized, and also the very fair detail in which he catalogues the booty.

It may be, however, that the power of the *Iliad* does not rest finally either on its theme or on its details as much as on the stark opening ('*in medias res*', as Horace comments) and the superb final books. If this power reminds us of Greek tragedy, it is as well to remind ourselves that Aeschylus is supposed to have called his plays 'slices from the great banquet of Homer'. The opening books are notable for their skill of exposition; in Book 1 the poet

introduces the theme of the anger of Achilles and describes th
attitudes adopted by the gods on Olympus; Book 2 describes th
Greek army after ten years of siege; Book 3 cleverly introduce
the Trojans by showing us the army of Book 2 through the eyes o
Helen (the cause of the war) and Priam. By the time of the fina
books, following the death of Hector, plot has given way to trag
intensity. In Book 22 Greece and Troy are balanced in the du
between Hector and Achilles. Book 23, the Funeral Games o
Patroclus, is entirely Greek. The final book ends the epic whic
began with Achilles by concentrating on what has become th
central tragedy, the dead Trojan, Hector. Priam approache
Achilles for permission to remove his son's body. Achille
reminded of his own father, joins Priam in his tears. The old kin
is allowed to carry the body to Troy, where it is greeted with
formal lament by the four ladies, Cassandra, Andromach
Hecuba and Helen, with her incomparable tribute to Hector. Th
epic closes with a simple account of the funeral, ending on th
cadence:

> These were the burial rites of Hector, tamer of horses.

There are few rivals to this 'dying fall' at the close of the *Iliad*
but the lines of *Beowulf* offer a similar experience:

> They said that of earthly kings
> he was the mildest and gentlest of men,
> kindest to his people, and the most eager for praise.

In this serenity we find another antidote to our casual belief tha
epic literature can only deal in massive effects.

Yet *Beowulf* shares all the heroic qualities of the *Iliad*, as can b
seen in the famous passage known as the Survivor's Lament:

> Guard now, o earth, the warriors' possessions
> when the heroes cannot. Yes, brave men took it from
> you before

a deadly evil, death in action, carried off
all the men of my people who left this life —
they had seen joy in the hall. No one to bear a sword
or polish the ornate vessel, the precious cup —
the old warriors have gone away.
The strong helmet adorned with gold
will be stripped of its beaten plates. They are asleep
those polishers who should make the war-mask gleam.
And the coat of mail that survived the bite of steel
as shields crashed in battle, that also decays
like the man who wore it. A coat of mail
cannot wander far and wide with heroes
after the warrior passes. No joy comes from the harp,
no mirth from the lyre, nor does the good hawk
circle the hall or the swift horse
stamp in the court. Baleful death
has sent away many generations of men.

(ll. 2247– 66)

We find here the same joy in the beauty of possessions, the same
intimate appreciation of the value of a fine weapon that is so
frequent in the *Iliad*. There is the same pleasure in the noise and
fury of warfare and the same love of animals for hunting, in this
case the hawk and the horse; the *Odyssey* often praises dogs for
their hunting ability.

Yet the passage also illustrates a fundamental difference between
the Homeric poems and the Anglo-Saxon. The former are noted
for their brightness, as if they were an expression in words of the
brilliant Greek sunlight. The language is open and explicit, the
images presented with total clarity, the mood, even in passages of
pathos, seldom gloomy. The comparison is made between the
Olympian religion which prevails in the poems, a religion of
mountains, air and light, and the dark cult of the earth-gods, the
Chthonic religion, which the Olympians largely supplanted. In
the *Odyssey* the central point, Book 11, describes the visit of
Odysseus to the Underworld in terms that remind us more of the

Chthonic cult; but otherwise very little disturbs the Olympi
mood, with one outstanding exception, in Book 20, when Penelo
announces her decision to marry one of the Suitors:

> And Pallas Athena aroused in the Suitors
> unquenchable laughter, and turned their minds.
> Then they were no longer laughing with their own mouths,
> and the meat they were eating ran with blood. Their eyes
> filled with tears and their hearts swelled with groans.
> Then the divine prophet Theoclymenus spoke to them:
> 'Ah wretches, what has become of you? Darkness
> flows over your heads and faces to your feet,
> the air blazes with shrieks, your cheeks drip tears,
> the walls and fine roof-beams run blood,
> gateway, passage and hall-way crowd with ghosts
> journeying to Hell mouth, the sun
> has vanished from the sky, and a vile mist covers everything.'
>
> (20, 345–5

W. B. Stanford comments: 'A very remarkable and macabre scen
its atmosphere has been compared to that of the Writing on t
Wall at Belshazzar's Feast and the apparition of Banquo at t
Banquet in *Macbeth*.'

In Homer, therefore, such dark passages are rare, and are a
the more striking when they occur; but in *Beowulf* darkne
provides one of the poem's main tensions, and pessimism and
sense of doom are its prevailing moods. The hero is engaged in
struggle with the powers of darkness, a struggle which must end
defeat and decay, but his heroism and later reputation depend upo
his conduct of the struggle. In the first half of the poem Beow
fights the monster Grendel and its mother, whose home is describ
in verses 1357B–1367:

> They guard a strange land,
> wolf-slopes, windy headlands,
> the terrible fen-path, where a mountain stream
> slides down below the mists of the crags –

a flood under the earth. Not many miles
from here that lake stands.
Groves covered with frost hang over it;
a firmly rooted wood overshadows the water.
Every night a fearful wonder can be seen —
fire on the flood. Of the children of men
no man alive is wise enough to know that land.

This is the landscape where Grendel (descended from the first murderer Cain) holds sway. The darkness which Beowulf fights may stand for the power of evil, but a primitive fear of the dark exists alongside the Christian allegory.

The epic of *Beowulf* begins with the funeral of Scyld Scefing, the legendary first king of the Danes, and ends with the funeral of Beowulf. Between these two points Beowulf first fights and kills Grendel and Grendel's mother, who had threatened the Danes, and then, after a prosperous reign, kills the Dragon of the Treasure, who had threatened his subjects, the Geats, and is himself killed in the fight. The structure is simple, but these four incidents contain a whole civilization. It is one of the characteristics of epic that it can contain great themes within simple frameworks, and this is as true of *Beowulf* as of the *Iliad*.

VIRGIL, *Aeneid*

About 25 B.C. Propertius wrote a poem in which he announced the approach of an exciting new work:

Nescio quid maius nascitur Iliade.

(Something greater than the *Iliad* has been conceived.)

The claim is simple, and total: there are no qualifications, no apologies; the new poem is better than Homer's. This must have been a profoundly shocking statement at a time when Homer's poems had stood unchallenged since the beginning of Roman literature, when Livius Andronicus had translated the *Odysse* Livius, a Greek of Tarentum, came to Rome as a slave, and w one of a long line of Greeks who imposed their culture on the conquerors. His translation of the *Odyssey*, made in the thi century B.C., was still a schoolbook in Vergil's day, and the ep itself had been venerated to the point of idolatry; disputes we settled by reference to the great poet's works, and an apt quotatic clinched any argument. Yet for all this, Vergil's rival productic was accepted almost immediately, and on Propertius' uncompron ising terms. Rome was certain that this poem did indeed surpa Homer, and the reason cannot have been mere chauvinism; the had been other epics, notably those of Naevius and Ennius, who *Annales* were greatly admired; but Ennius seems to have be revered as an original poet of great stature, the 'father of Lat poetry', rather than as a rival to Homer. Vergil's claim rests on t fact that he challenged Homer on his own territory.

Yet there is one crucial difference between Vergil and Home which is summed up in the critical terms 'primary' and 'secondary 'oral' and 'literary'. The American critic Brooks Otis closes h book on Vergil with the statement:

> In a word, Vergil is a civilized poet. By comparison Homer is prim tive or barbarous. This fact has usually been admitted in greater lesser degree, but usually also with the implication that Homer w *therefore* the greater poet. . . . Vergil's greatness consists precisely his ability to make civilization poetical.

(*Vergil, A Study in Civilized Poetry*, p. 39

Resembling in this matter more the Old Testament than the *Ilic* or *Odyssey*, the *Aeneid* is written with a strong sense of nation identity and destiny – so strong, in fact, that it has been calle 'nationalistic' and 'propagandist' by its detractors, who inclue such eminent modern poets as Pound, Auden and Graves. In t amusing poem 'Secondary Epic' from *Homage to Clio* (196 Auden notes that in the description of the shield of Aeneas whic

ıds Book 8 the great tableau closes abruptly with the battle of
ctium in 31 B.C.:

> No, Vergil, no:
>   Not even the first of the Romans can learn
> His Roman history in the future tense,
>   Not even to serve your political turn;
> Hindsight as foresight makes no sense.

uden has fixed on the poem's greatest weaknesses; it is a com-
ıissioned epic, written for Augustus and his court; and it is written
ı the assumption that Augustan Rome stood at the apex of Roman
story, for which previous events had been only a preparation.
ergil and Horace wrote with such urbanity and power that this
logical view has been widely accepted and taught, despite the
ear fact that the Civil War destroyed a distinctive Republican
ılture which boasted Lucretius, Catullus, Caesar and Cicero as its
pical examples, broadminded, subversive, exploratory. The
riters of the early Empire, on the other hand, are more aware of
ıeir duty to Rome and the Emperor, rather too eager to compose
celebration ode or panegyric, rather too dependent on patronage
ı 'rock the boat' too vigorously.

This is the worse side of the coin; despite these flaws, the poem
mains one of the great achievements of European poetry; and
is obviously in the classical epic tradition. There is first of all
ıe single, monolithic hero, Aeneas, a man of Destiny, who leads
small band of Trojans from burning Troy to found a new city on
ıe banks of the Tiber, as he says in an early speech to his followers
a moment of crisis:

> Some day we may remember this also with joy.
> After so many trials and tricks of Fortune
> we press on to Latium, a promised haven;
> there is the place for Troy's new empire to grow.
>   (*Aeneid* 1, 203–6)

This great central figure of 'pius Aeneas' stands out (as Odysseus did) against the tableau of the collapse of Troy's empire. The Fall of Troy is told early in the work, in Book 2, the most immediately attractive of the poem, with all the colour and excitement of a boy's adventure story and at the same time the 'dying fall' found at the close of the *Iliad* and in the great tragedies.

The fall of one civilization is paralleled in the poem by the rise of another. In Book 1 Aeneas sees the growing walls of the new city of Carthage and envies its citizens (line 437); the longing for a new city pervades the whole poem until the final lines, when the last obstacles are removed, and the foundation of Rome becomes a possibility. There is no epic with a hero so isolated and so explicitly a representative of a civilization.

The style and method of the poem also hark back to Homer. It has often been noted that the first six books, the wandering of the Trojans, correspond to the *Odyssey*, as the wars in Latium correspond to the *Iliad*. Both halves begin with an invocation; there are notable digressions (including the shield of Aeneas in Book 8 already mentioned, which corresponds to Homer's description of the Shield of Achilles in *Iliad* 18 – the subject of another fine poem by Auden); and as might be expected Vergil makes good use of the simile, the most easily recognized of epic devices. The *Aeneid* uses proportionally more than the *Odyssey* and fewer than the *Iliad* (which with its many similar battle-scenes encourages the use of similes for variety and interest). Yet nothing more clearly demonstrates the difference between the two authors than a study of their similes. We have seen how in the Homeric poems the author, delighting in the simile, follows its details for their own sake. Vergil rarely does this. For him all the details comment directly on the object described by the simile. He is certainly a more conscious artist; it may be that we see here also the difference between oral and written poetry. In Book 13 of the *Iliad* Idomeneus kills Asius (line 388) with a spear thrust:

The bronze passed straight through his throat, under the chin.
He fell, as an oak falls or a poplar,
or a tall pine which the woodsmen fell on the hills
with their sharp axes, to build a ship.

The pictures are quite dissimilar – the spear pierces, the axe chops; an oak describes a warrior considerably better than a poplar or pine can; the ship is almost an afterthought.

Vergil borrows the simile at the moment of Troy's fall in *Aeneid* 2:

Then, then, I seemed to see Ilium come to its knees
in the flames, and Neptune's Troy toppled.
Just like an old ash-tree on the highest mountain –
the farmers hack at it with a rain of blows
from their double-axes. The tree totters,
trembling it nods its leaves and quivering top branches,
until, worn out with wounds, it gives a last groan
and falls headlong, with a crash, in ruins.

(2, 624–31)

Here there are so many descriptive words which could refer to the ash or the besieged city, some of them almost more apt for the city. Image and theme are fused together, linked almost organically, to produce a rich texture with infinite echoes and associations. The contrast may again be made by quoting another simile from Homer, vivid and colourful as the first, but no more integrated with the subject. It accompanies the death of Simoisius in *Iliad* 4:

And he fell in the dust like a poplar
growing up tall in the open water-meadows,
slim, but topped with bushy foliage.
A wainwright chops it down with his bright axe
to carve out a rim for the wheel of a fine chariot,
and leaves it to season by the river-bank.

The quality that distinguishes the *Aeneid* from all other epics is its sense of the past. In this its closest rival is *Beowulf* with its brooding fens and monsters. The *Aeneid*, despite its civilized form and

c

language, reaches on occasion into the darkest recesses of the mind to produce not Gothic horror, but a sense of awe and mystery. On such moment is found in Book 6, the Descent into the Under world, a parallel with *Odyssey* 11, the core of that poem also. On his journey through the Underworld Aeneas is told to look for the Golden Bough, the key to the lower world. If he is called by the Fates the bough will be picked easily. Aeneas finds it, and pluck it without effort. C. S. Lewis comments on this section of the poem:

> I do not know of a better example of imagination, in the highest sense than when Charon wonders at the Golden Bough 'so long unseen' dark centuries of that unhistoried lower world are conjured up in half a line (6, 409).

(*A Preface to Paradise Lost*, p. 36)

The construction of the poem as a whole appears to be based on a pattern of peaks and valleys, with the comparatively lower-key books, One, Three and Five preparing for the climaxes, the Fall of Troy in Book Two, the tragedy of Dido in Four, the Descent to the Underworld in Six. Of all the outstanding passages in these three books there can be few more central to Vergil's thought than the lines in which Anchises analyses the function of Rome as an imperial power:

> Greece will cast breathing likenesses in bronze
> and chisel living faces out of stone
> give others greater eloquence at law, or follow
> the sweep of the planets and the cycle of stars
> but remember, Rome, to rule your empire,
> impose the custom of peace (your particular skill)
> generous always in victory, ruthless against pride.

(6, 847–53)

It is passages of this kind which lead C. S. Lewis to the judgement that

> With Vergil European poetry grows up.

OVID, *Metamorphoses*

When Vergil was on his deathbed in 19 B.C. he gave instructions for the *Aeneid* to be burnt. He had worked on the poem for eleven years, but it still lacked the final polish, for which he had planned a further three years' work. His instructions were ignored. Twenty-five years after the death of Vergil, Ovid was banished to the shores of the Black Sea for an unknown offence, perhaps connected with the Emperor's family. One of his last acts in Rome was to burn his manuscripts of his *Metamorphoses*; one strongly suspects that he had made certain that there were two or three copies of the work in circulation. At all events, the poem survived; but the gesture had been made – Ovid had invited comparison with Vergil, just as Vergil had with Homer.

The difficulty is in knowing at what point any comparison can usefully be made. Lemprière, in his *Classical Dictionary* (1788), one of the books that Keats knew almost by heart, states plainly:

> His *Metamorphoses*, in fifteen books, are extremely curious, on account of the many different facts and traditions which they relate, but they can have no claim to be an epic poem.

Ovid, however, was quite certain that he was writing an epic. He simply changed the rules of the epic to suit the work that he was composing. When one notes that his first change was to abandon the idea of the hero, it becomes clear how great a change he was prepared to make. The fact that it contains more similes than the *Iliad*, despite being over three thousand lines shorter, is an indication of how traditional he was prepared to be in those areas where he was not innovating. The poem has, in fact, all the characteristics of epic style: it is written in hexameters; it has invocations to the gods; it has similes; its tone is at times expansive, at times exalted; and, above all, it is full of digressions.

The intention behind the poem can be expressed quite simply.

It is a collection in verse of almost every known myth, beginning with the Creation and Flood, and ending with the transformation of the dead Julius Caesar into a comet. The unity of the poem consists in the fact that all the myths chosen contain some transformation or metamorphosis. There is finally a general organization of the myths into three categories, Gods, Heroes and Men, each taking up approximately one third of the work.

To this bald statement of the poem's characteristics there must be added an essential ingredient: the poet's outstanding virtuosity. The myths are intertwined with an intricacy and variety that is more reminiscent of a nineteenth-century novel than of a Latin poem. Ovid delights in such devices as placing one story inside another, in allusive transitions from one tale to the next, in the unusual and bizarre wherever he finds it. In its intricacy the closest parallels in poetry might be Spenser and his fellow-Elizabethans. Certainly Arthur Golding's translation published in 1567 is at the centre of Elizabethan classicism; the *Metamorphoses* are among the major influences on Renaissance poetry; and the metaphor which springs most easily to mind to describe them, a vast tapestry, is characteristic of the Renaissance. L. P. Wilkinson gives an excellent description:

> Yes, the *Metamorphoses* is 'baroque' in conception with its huge extent of ceaseless movement (like the Pergamene frieze of battling gods and giants), its variety, its fantasy, its conceits and shocks, its penchant for the grotesque and its blend of humour and grandiosity.
>
> (*Ovid Recalled*, p. 159)

Yet there is a still more meaningful critical adjective available to describe the *Metamorphoses*: 'Alexandrian'. The Hellenistic poets had as great an impact on Rome as any previous writers, and it is from the Hellenistic tradition that the characteristic attention to detail and psychological awareness of the best Latin poetry stems. Hellenistic art has often been called 'decadent' by comparison with the sculptures of Phidias and the plays of Aeschylus in the fifth century, but it was in fact the most cultured of ages, and the library at Alexandria, until its destruction by fire during the siege of the city by Julius Caesar, was the greatest in the Western world.

Three relationships in particular between Hellenistic poets and Roman are of great importance. The *Argonautica* of Apollonius Rhodius, a hexameter epic closely imitating Homer, profoundly influenced Vergil's *Aeneid*. In particular the treatment of Medea by Apollonius, with its great depth of characterization and sympathy (Apollonius himself surely influenced in this by Euripides) provided much of the basis for the superb portrait of Dido in *Aeneid* 4. The relationship between the *Coma Berenices* of Callimachus (with its Latin version by Catullus at his most Alexandrian) and Pope's *Rape of the Lock* will be discussed in a later chapter. But the most pervasive of the three influences is that of the *Aetia* of Callimachus, of which the *Coma* is a small section. The 'elaborate and erudite *Aetia*' as Wilkinson calls it survives only in fragments, but in its conception and execution it is obviously the forerunner of Ovid's work. Callimachus himself has behind him the great figure of Hesiod, whose *Works and Days* were considered almost contemporary with Homer's poems. But the *Works and Days*, while vivid and charming, are more a didactic work on agriculture than an epic, and are closer to Vergil's *Georgics* or Spenser's *Shepherd's Calendar* than to Homer. The *Aetia*, however, appear to have the sweep and purpose of an epic poem.

Each action is a story explaining the origin of some existing name or legend, and the parts are linked together with very much the same ingenuity that Ovid brings to his task. His tones range as widely as Ovid's, the styles vary as strikingly. Most of all Ovid borrows from Callimachus (as Vergil had from Apollonius) his fascinated attention to unusual detail; and this is nowhere better illustrated than in a famous episode in Book 3, in which the god

Bacchus, kidnapped by a crew of Lydian sailors, changes them
into dolphins:

> The ship sticks in the water
> just as if it were stowed in dry dock;
> the startled sailors redouble their oar-strokes
> and hoist all sail, looking for extra power;
> but ivy tendrils clog the oars, creeping and twisting,
> and adorn the sails with heavy bunches.
> Bacchus himself, his brows hung with berry-clusters,
> shakes a spear wreathed in ivy-leaves;
> around him lie sprawled the ghost shapes
> of tigers, lynxes and savage spotted panthers.
> The sailors jump overboard, propelled
> either by madness or fear; but first Medon
> feels his body darken, his spine bend into a curve.
> Says Lycabas: 'What weird monster are you becoming?'
> And as he speaks his jaws fix in a grin,
> his nose arches, his skin hardens into scales.
> Libys, tugging at the stubborn oar,
> sees his hands shorten till they become
> not hands at all, but should be called fins.
> Another, trying to catch at the twisted ropes
> finds he has no hands and arches backwards
> limbless into the sea; the end of his tail
> sickle-shaped, like the curve of the half-moon.
> Their leaps send up showers and spatters of spray
> as they burst from the sea and plunge in again
> like a troupe of dancers, gambolling in sport
> and spraying out what they inhale with their wide nostrils.
> Of the twenty men (the ship had held that number
> a moment before) there was I, alone.

(3, 660–88

The writing is wonderfully vivid, from the similes (the ship i
dry dock, the troupe of dancers) to the observant adjectives (th
startled sailors, the ghost shapes of the wild beasts, the twisted

opes), but most admirable are the details which come not from observation but imagination; Medon sees his body darken, Libys sees his hands shorten, the narrator's first thought on finding himself alone, is to calculate how many men have been transformed in so short a time. The emphasis is on reality, closeness to life, and every detail is chosen for its immediacy and freshness. It is easy to see why the Renaissance picked so readily on Ovid to express for them the vitality of their newly discovered world. The 'Alexandrian' or 'baroque' elements in the passage are equally plain, the conscious variation (each sailor is transformed in a different manner), the ornateness of description (the clustering vine-foliage, the almost architectural curves and volutes, the showers of spray); but above all we are struck by the interest shown in the human actors in the story, and in their reactions to their own transformations. It is almost as if Ovid is obsessed, throughout his epic, with the single image of a person observing with horror (or interest?) the gradual transformation of his body into something else.

There is an even more celebrated episode, the metamorphosis of Daphne into a laurel (1, 548 ff.):

> Almost in mid-prayer a heavy numbness fills her limbs,
> her soft flanks are encased with thin bark,
> her hair grows into leaves, her arms into branches,
> her foot, just in full flight, sticks in sluggish roots,
> and her head has a bushy top. Only the skin's gleam is left.
>
> Apollo loves the tree as well; pressing the trunk with his hand
> he can feel the heart still fluttering under the new bark. . . .

The humour here is intentional, just as the grotesquerie of the dolphins had been; but alongside the humour is a sense of the reality of the occasion (how many other authors would have the god feel the girl's heart pulsing even after the transformation into a tree?) which makes the moment unforgettable. In fact, Ovid's intensity of interest created one of the most popular images of the Renaissance, inspiring a painting by Pollaiuolo, now in the

National Gallery, and a sculpture by Bernini. Petrarch ofte
referred to the episode; and Rinuccini, writing the libretto for th
first opera, in 1594, used the story of Apollo and Daphne. There i
nothing surprising in the popularity of the episode – the compariso
of a girl with a tree is one of the most deep-seated of poeti
images – but it is a tribute to the versatility of Ovid's poem that i
can accommodate easily as a single episode what would for anothe
author become the subject of a complete work.

This, then, is Ovid's answer to Vergil; and while they lack th
majesty of Vergil's poem, the *Metamorphoses* are a gigantic strid
forward. In abandoning the central hero and finding instead
loose framework which could accommodate almost any materi
that came to hand, Ovid paved the way for Dante and man
modern writers, notably Ezra Pound. Vergil had given the epi
psychological depth; Ovid reshaped it to give it infinite scope.

LUCAN, *Pharsalia*

When Lucan died aged 26 in A.D. 65, by order of Nero, he le
behind him the first ten books of a perverse and infuriating epic o
the Civil War between Caesar and Pompey. It is hard to admir
the *Pharsalia*, but impossible to ignore it.

The poet, born in Cordova, was a provincial, like his com
patriot Martial and the North Italians Catullus and Vergil. Hi
uncle, Seneca, was one of the greatest intellects of his day, and th
poet clearly learnt from him his considerable verbal expertise
More important, however, than either his Spanish blood or hi
early rhetorical training was his youth; the *Pharsalia* is a youn
man's epic. Marlowe began a translation of the poem; Shelle
joined Lucan with Chatterton and Sidney in his *Adonais* as

> inheritors of unfulfilled renown.

The poem is remarkable for its contrasts, the constant use o hyperbole side by side with the most arresting epigrams. An extended passage in Book 9 describes the horrors experienced by Cato's soldiers in the deserts of Libya, in particular a bewildering variety of poisonous snakes. The effect produced by the bite of one of these, the *haemorrhois*, is described by Lucan as follows:

> His tears were blood. From every gate of his body
> the blood flowed freely. His mouth was filled with it
> and his flared nostrils. He sweated crimson. In every limb
> his brimming veins overflowed. He was all one wound.
>
> (9, 811–14)

In passages of this kind Lucan is clearly making no effort to challenge Vergil in the field which Tennyson's 'lord of language' had made his own. Vergil's art is to choose every word for its precise effect and meaning, while at the same time preserving

> the stateliest measure
> ever moulded by the lips of man.
>
> (Tennyson, *To Virgil*)

Lucan is prepared to sacrifice everything, logic, verbal beauty, even common sense, for the sake of the single memorable picture of a dying soldier. Economy and understatement have no place in the poem. It is a miracle that this extended display of verbal fireworks could be moulded into anything resembling an epic.

Yet it clearly is an epic. In purely formal terms Lucan has based his work on his most classical predecessors; the poem deals with a heroic theme in past history; it was intended to have a twelve-book structure; invocations, similes, digressions, are all used freely. Line by line, it is not like any other classical epic; taken as a whole, it can be nothing else.

These are the faults of the *Pharsalia*; it is impetuous, melodramatic, shrill. Yet it is by no means without subtlety. Soon after the description of Cato's experiences in Libya there follows an account of Caesar's visit to the site of Troy, which gives an indication of the quality of Lucan's best writing. The passage begins quietly, with a nostalgic revisiting of the familiar names of Homer's poems. As the guided tour continues, however, we realize that we are reading an early satire on the trade in bogus antiquities until with the final outburst the tone descends to total sarcasm:

> Caesar, that lover of greatness, explores the sands of Sigeum,
> the river Simois, Rhoetium, marked by the tomb
> of Greek Ajax, and the dead who owe everything to Homer.
> He walks around charred Troy (now only a name)
> searching for the massive remnants of Apollo's walls.
> Now barren woods and rotting stumps of trees
> bear down on the palace of Assaracus, and tired roots
> strangle the gods' temples, while the whole citadel
> is a mass of brambles. The very ruins are in ruins.
> He gazes at Hesione's rock, and the wooded grotto
> where Venus visited Anchises. Here is the cave where Paris
> sat to give judgement, here Ganymede was snatched off to heaven,
> the Naiad Oenone wept here. There is a sermon in every stone.
> Without thinking, he stepped across a dusty trickle;
> it was the Xanthus. Carelessly, he put down his foot
> in the long grass. His native guide advised him
> not to tread on the bones of Hector. Some scattered stones
> lay in disorder, desecrated. 'What?' said the guide,
> 'Are you passing by the altar of Zeus?'
>
> How divine and awesome the work of poets! They alone
> snatch the world from Fate and give mortals immortality!
>
> (9, 961–81)

Vergil and Ovid were both innovators; Vergil with his majestic conflation of *Iliad* and *Odyssey* into one poem, and Ovid in that unique, sprawling collection of anecdotes. But Lucan in full stride with his eye fixed on the object of his satire, is a formidable competitor. Quintilian, another Spaniard, describes him best:

> Lucan, fiery, vigorous, master of epigram.

3
New Form

In the middle of the fourteenth century Petrarch, today best known for his lyric poems in Italian, wrote a Latin epic, *Africa*, dealing with the struggle between Rome and Carthage, which he believed would be the basis of his fame. In that crucial early phase of the renaissance of the Greek and Latin Classics Petrarch, as a fine classical scholar, pinned his faith on Latin as the language for major poetry; his personal poems could be in the vernacular, but his monumental work, on which his reputation was to rest, had to be in Latin. Looking back with hindsight on this period, we admire the scholar and the lyric poet, but cannot see his epic as rivalling those of Vergil or Lucan. He was a master of the sonnet and canzone, which were to have such an influence on European literature; but as an epic poet he had already been superseded by almost half a century. Soon after 1300, Dante had begun to write his *Divina Commedia*, in Italian.

It was apparently the poet Guido Cavalcanti, 'my best friend', as Dante calls him in the *Vita Nuova*, who suggested that Dante write in Italian rather than Latin, and these two poets now stand at the head of the vernacular tradition of love poetry later carried forward by Petrarch. Another passage in the *Vita Nuova*, chapter 9, describes the writing of Dante's First Canzone, 'Donne, ch'avete intelletto d'Amore' ('Ladies, you who have knowledge of Love'), a lyrical description of this lady, Beatrice, in the form of an address to her friends. This canzone had immediate success; in Canto 24 of *Purgatorio* Dante describes his meeting with a rival

poet, Bonagiunta of Lucca, who asks if the man whom he see
before him

> Invented those new rhymes that begin:
> 'Ladies, you who have knowledge of Love.'
>
> (*Purgatorio* 24, 5c

Clearly this was one of the best appreciated of the poems writte
before the *Divina Commedia*. Dante's reply to the question i
revealing:

> I am a man who takes note
> when love inspires me, and as he dictates,
> that is the way that I write.

Bonagiunta reacts with a famous judgement – at last he realize
what it was that kept himself and his fellow-poets from achievin
the 'sweet new style' ('il dolce stil nuovo') which was the hall
mark of Dante and his fellow Florentine, Cavalcanti. In this shor
exchange both sides of Dante's excellence are described, hi
revolutionary new style, and his equally revolutionary use of Lov
as his central subject. For in Dante's poetry Love is not a synonyr
for affection, but for Christ himself.

It is through this that we discover the secret of the remarkabl
unity of the *Commedia*. The poem begins 'In the middle way of ou
life', plunges into the funnel of Inferno, climbs the cone whic
answers to the funnel, the Mount of Purgatory, to the Earthl
Paradise at its summit. from which the poet ascends through th
Ten Heavens, past the

> Thrones, Dominations, Princedoms, Virtues, Powers,

to a vision of God in the final canto. This vast conception is mad
possible by two things, the reader's identification with the centra
character, Dante himself, and more importantly, the reader'
understanding of a central theme, Love.

This theme is introduced at once in the meeting of Dante with Vergil:

> O first of poets, their greatest light,
>> may I be blessed for the love and studious care
>> which made me search your volume out.
>
> You are my master and my author,
>> you alone the one from whom I took
>> the fine style that has done me honour.
>
> (Inferno 1, 82–7)

Dante's love for Vergil as a poet leads us on to his idealized love for Beatrice, whom he meets in Canto 30 of *Purgatorio*. Dante is so overcome by the vision that he turns for help to Vergil, but finds him gone. Beatrice consoles him for his loss in words that are among the most striking and mysterious in the poem, and contain the only mention of the poet's name in the work:

> Dante, because Vergil has disappeared
>> do not weep, do not weep yet
>> for you must weep for another sword.
>
> (Purgatorio 30, 55–7)

The sequence of thought, however, is not complete. Already in the *Vita Nuova* Dante had equated Beatrice with Christ. Now the correlation is almost explicit as she becomes his guide through the Heavens to the Throne of God, and there presents him to the Creator, who is Pure Love. We feel irresistibly in the final cantos that this is the only possible culmination of a line of argument that began with the opening words of the poem.

It is not solely a philosophical poem, however, nor is its subject-matter as single-handed as this brief summary suggests. The technique of the first three lines of the *Commedia* give some indication of its poetic power:

> Nel mezzo del cammin di nostra vita
> mi ritrovai per una selva oscura
> che la diritta via era smarrita.

> (In the middle of our life's road
> I came to myself in a dark wood
> where the straight way had disappeared.)

In the first line the literal meaning must be that the poet was aged thirty-five, half of the traditional life-span of 'three score years and ten'; but the metaphor of the 'way of life' has equally strong humanist and religious associations. Similarly, the second line sets the scene for any one of a thousand romantic tales: 'Once upon a time a knight was riding through a dark forest.' In Dante's words, however, there is something which tells us that we are not reading a romance. They remind us more of the dark forest at the centre of *Gilgamesh*. The third line reinforces this feeling of duality: the hero has strayed from the direct way; the words again hover between pure narrative and religious allegory. After only three lines it is clear that this is a new kind of work, the earliest epic written in the first person. Clearly the seeds of this development had always been present in epic writing; the close concentration upon the central figure, and the implication of the whole of life continuing in the background, had always allowed of the possibility of a detailed analysis of the hero's soul. By comparison with Odysseus, where our interest is held by Homer's minute observation of the man as he is, we begin to see in Vergil's Aeneas a greater interest in psychology. The external details in Homer of dress and appearance, of action and reaction, are in some degree replaced in Vergil by an interest in motivation and sensitivity summed up in the famous line

> sunt lacrimae rerum, et mentem mortalia tangunt

> (there are tears in things, and the world touches the mind.)

In Dante, however, the poet of an Italy still largely unaffected by the humanist renaissance, the centre of his epic was the soul, and its theme the journey of that soul towards a revelation of Divine Love. There is a sense in which the *Divina Commedia* is closer to the Myth of Er at the end of Plato's *Republic* or to the *Apocalypse* of St John at the end of the New Testament than it is to the *Odyssey* and the *Aeneid*.

Yet the greatness of Dante's poem lies in the fact that this weight of allegory and philosophy is easily assimilated into one of the most rapid and compellingly narrated stories in Western literature. In canto after canto we are led deeper and deeper into Purgatory, then to soar upwards into the light with a breathtaking urgency; and the whole route is lined with every possible variation of human character, exemplified in the famous names of the past. It is hard to think of a significant historical figure absent from Dante's poem. The poet's predecessors are prominent:

> There is Homer, prince of the poets,
>   Horace the satirist comes next,
>   the third is Ovid, and Lucan the last.
>
> (*Inferno* 4, 88 ff.)

Vergil, of course, is at his shoulder. The heroes of Troy are there also, and those of medieval romance. More than anything, however, we find in the poem the most vivid picture of medieval Italy. Hundreds of Dante's contemporaries and near contemporaries are shown, from the heretical Popes to Francesca of Rimini, whose tragic love of Paolo took place in Dante's own lifetime. The description of the two lovers in *Inferno* 5, swept by the wind of passion, and Paolo's tears as Francesca tells their story, is a heartrending moment. At the other extreme is the horror of the traitors frozen into eternal ice at the depths of Inferno, among them Ugolino and Ruggieri, gnawing in hunger at each other's heads projecting from the solid ice.

In one passage of the *Inferno*, however, the classical and the medieval, the nostalgic and the exploratory, are drawn together into a magical speech that is entirely Dante's invention. At the close of Canto 26 the poets persuade Ulysses to tell his story, and the greatest wanderer describes his last journey, out beyond the Pillars of Hercules and across the Equator, until he and his companions catch sight of the Mount of Purgatory in the distance, moments before their ship is overwhelmed:

> Then turning our prow towards the morning
>   we used our oars as wings to fly
>   and on our left we were still gaining,
>
> Till night showed us the other pole in the sky
>   and ours sank down so low
>   that it could hardly lift itself from the sea.
>
> And the moon's torch had lost its glow,
>   five times rekindled, five times dwindled away
>   since my tired sailors had begun to row
>
> When there appeared a Mountain, grey
>   from the distance, and it seemed more tall
>   than any I had seen before that day
>
> And we rejoiced, but soon our spirits fell
>   as a whirlwind came out of the new land
>   and struck the foremost planks of our hull.
>
> Three times in those great waves it spun us round
>   and at the fourth the stern rose
>   and, as it pleased Him, the prow plunged down
>
> And the sea met once again above us.

(*Inferno* 26, 91–142)

In this passage there is a sense of destiny that we rarely feel with Homer's Odysseus. Erich Auerbach says of the poem (in *Dante: Poet of the Secular World*) that 'With Dante, the historical individual was reborn in his manifest unity of body and spirit; he was both old and new, rising from long oblivion with greater power and scope than ever before.' The *Divina Commedia* established the personal epic; a new dimension had been added which would make Petrarch's pastiche of Vergil sadly irrelevant before it had even been written; with this single leap of the imagination poets were now able to write epic poems on ideas and themes which had previously been handled in lyrics. The *Divina Commedia* makes possible Wordsworth's *Prelude* and Pound's *Cantos*.

LANGLAND AND CHAUCER

Emerson says of Dante, in his essay 'The Poet', 'Dante's praise is, that he dared to write his autobiography in colossal cypher, or into universality.' This brief judgement sums up the importance of Dante in the epic tradition. The *Commedia* was so individual and personal that it compelled his successors to halt and think again about the function of epic; this may be the correct moment in a critical study to pause and take stock also.

The medieval writer could look back on a whole range of classical epic, though he would certainly not have been influenced by all the writers equally. The list included Homer, whom he might well not have read either in Greek or in translation, Vergil, who was credited with almost magical power, and also an author of little importance to classical literature but of great popularity later, Statius. His best poems, elegant and courtly pieces for his friends (one of them Lucan) are excellent of their kind; but his epic, the *Thebaid*, on the theme of the *Seven Against Thebes*, is a somewhat pedestrian and derivative work, without either the inventiveness of Lucan or the originality of Ovid. It was popular in the Middle Ages as a storehouse of fables told in a vivid (if sometimes grossly overstated) manner. The story in Chaucer's *Knight's Tale*, the rivalry of Palamon and Arcite for the love of Emelye, came through Boccaccio, from the *Thebaid*.

It is at first sight surprising that Statius, the least original of epic writers, should have been among the most popular, until one realizes how unimportant the notion of 'originality' was to the medieval writer. He was much more likely, indeed, to invent a non-existent source than to claim originality. In his *Troylus and Criseyde* (1, 394) Chaucer offers as his source

> myn auctor called Lollius

despite the fact that no such author existed; Chaucer has misunderstood a line in Horace's *Epistles*; his true source was the *Filostrato* of Boccaccio.

In this kind of literary climate, of learning not altogether digested, and of models chosen for the worst rather than the best reasons, an epic such as Dante's provides both a turning-point and a challenge; and the period which followed was as experimental in the field of epic as in science. On the one hand there is the gradual growth of classical scholarship, culminating in the greatest age of English translation (the *Aeneid* of Gavin Douglas, Golding's *Metamorphoses*, Chapman's *Iliad*, Sir John Harington's Ariosto and finally Dryden's *Aeneid* and Pope's *Iliad*), while on the other we see a number of poets trying their hand at the epic form, with greater and lesser degrees of originality; of these, two names stand out, Spenser the contemporary of Chapman, and Milton, who was visited by the younger poet Dryden.

Yet Spenser and Milton wrote with a knowledge of Homer as well as of Vergil. In the fourteenth century, when such knowledge was uncertain, if it existed at all, two authors, Langland and Chaucer, produced poems which were quite unlike classical epic, but show many of the qualities, and certainly have the scope, of epic works. William Langland's *Vision of Piers Plowman* is very much a medieval poem; its style is that of alliteration, in imitation of the Old English of *Beowulf*:

In a summer seson when softe was the sunne,
I schop me into a schroud a scheep as I were;
In habit of an hermit unholy of werkes,
Went I wide in this world wondres to heare.
But in a Mayes morning on Malverne hilles
Me befell . . .

and he goes on to tell of a dream in which he sees a series of visions of working men, to make up a mixture of allegory and social satire. The whole poem is a vivid picture of the country life of the time, and was referred to by John Ball in his letter to the peasants of Essex during the Peasants' Revolt. Most importantly, in his freedom from classical models Langland found a form for his long poem strikingly similar to Dante's in its looseness of structure. The large canvas, the life of England in the 1360s, the vivid detailing inside it, together with the Ploughman hero (who by the end of the poem has become a Christ-figure), make up a work which, although not overtly epic, is an important contribution to the tradition of the long poem in English, which at its best is as all-inclusive as Ovid's or Dante's epic.

Chaucer's *Canterbury Tales* have no more claim than Langland's poem to be classed as a conventional epic, but they are another major contribution to the tradition. Chaucer's work has a different kind of unity from Langland's. The poem gathers a large variety of characters together by the simple device of having them all on a pilgrimage to Canterbury, during which each pilgrim was to tell two pairs of stories to beguile the time. The result is a long poem with a distinct oral character – one remembers that Homer's epics in particular contain large areas of poetry where the protagonists converse (and tell the story) in long speeches – and again the poet has found a loose structure which will accommodate every contemporary class and custom. The *Tales* also constitute a journey, not only the journey to Canterbury but also the development of Chaucer's final years; the twenty-three tales that were completed can be read as a diary of Chaucer's moods over those years. Just as Dante's great poem reflects his changing emotions as he remembers that single blinding vision in 1300, so Chaucer relives the short imaginary journey which began on that spring day in 1387,

> Whan that Aprille with his shoures soote
> The droghte of March hath perced to the roote . . .

Like *Piers Plowman*, the *Canterbury Tales* would not be placed in the central line of epic, but looking back from the twentieth century it is tempting to class Chaucer with Ovid and Dante in the tradition of the open, all-embracing narrative which, in the hands of William Carlos Williams, Pound, Eliot and David Jones has had such a successful recent history.

4
Renaissance and Later Epic

SPENSER, THE FAERIE QUEENE

Ben Jonson's characteristically grudging comment on Shakespeare's 'small *Latine,* and lesse *Greeke*' obscures an important truth, that whatever Shakespeare's classical learning (and he went to an excellent grammar school) and Jonson's scholarship (for he quotes a disturbing amount from handbooks of classical tags) the intuitive Shakespeare of *Julius Caesar* and *Antony and Cleopatra,* delicately steering a parallel course to North's Plutarch, leaves in the shade Jonson's pedantic *Catiline,* a tissue of direct quotations from Cicero painstakingly identified in the margin. In 1767 Richard Farmer, Master of Emmanuel College, published an important paper analysing the kind of use made by Shakespeare of translations of the classics rather than the originals. The reason for this was not so much weakness on Shakespeare's part, as the very high quality of the translations available – a similar situation has been the influence on modern poets of the excellent translations from the Chinese by Arthur Waley and Ezra Pound.

We know that Arthur Golding's *Metamorphoses,* published in 1567, was one of Shakespeare's favourite books. A passage from the beginning of Book 3, describing the serpent killed by Cadmus, illustrates the power which must have attracted the Elizabethan poets:

> The specled serpent straight
> Comes trailing out in waving linkes and knottie rolles of scales,
> And bending into bunchie boughts his bodie forth he hales.
> And lifting up above the wast himself unto the Skie
> He overlooketh all the wood; . . .

The vividness of description, with its awesome final line, and the strong rhythms (accentuated by alliteration, never quite overdone) find clear echoes in Elizabethan drama. The metre is the 'fourteener', the long line which Chapman also used in the translation of the *Iliad* which so impressed Keats on his first reading of it. Here is the death of Polydorus in Book 20:

> . . . he flew before the first heate of the field
> Even till he flew out of breath and soul – which, through the back,
> > the lance
> Of swift Achilles put in ayre, and did the head advance
> Out at his navill. On his knee the poor Prince fell,
> And gathered with his tender hands his entrails, and did swell
> Quite through the wide wound, till a cloud as blacke as death
> > concealed
> Their sight and all the world for him.

Quoting this passage in *Poetry* (Chicago), October, 1957, William Carlos Williams comments: 'That's straight talking, with a compelling vigour of phrase that has brought Chapman the attention and admiration of the ages.' Chapman's translation came thirty years after Golding's, and it can be seen how much more smoothly and less heavily accented the verse form is.

In the style of his epic, the *Faerie Queene*, Spenser certainly owes something to Golding and Chapman:

> But all those pleasant bowres and Pallace brave,
> > *Guyon* broke downe, with rigour pittilesse;
> > Ne ought their goodly workmanship might save
> > Them from the tempest of his wrathfulnesse,
> > But that their blisse he turn'd to balefulnesse:
> > Their groves he feld, their gardins did deface,
> > Their arbers spoyle, their Cabinets suppresse,
> > Their banket houses burne, their buildings race,
> And of the fairest late, now made the fowlest place.
>
> (II, 12, 83)

This moves along with the rapidity which one expects from good Elizabethan writing, but at the same time the beat is there, accentuated by the alliteration in almost every line; Spenser would have made a magnificent translation of *Beowulf*. The groves and arbours, however, and the 'fairest' of the final line, give the clue that this is not altogether in the Homeric mould, but follows at the same time the great parallel tradition of romance. The *Faerie Queene* is the first major work to combine romance and epic successfully.

The title-page gives a further clue: THE FAERIE QUEENE. Disposed into twelve bookes, Fashioning XII Morall vertues. Here again is the duality between romance (epitomized in the single word 'Faerie') and epic, clearly signalled by the Vergilian twelve book structure, (half of Homer's twenty-four) which became the pattern for conventional epic. The 'XII Morall vertues' are a third link in the chain, neither epic nor romance; The *Faerie Queene* is one of the great works of allegory. Writing to Sir Walter Raleigh when only the first three books were completed (out of the seven which were finally written) Spenser begins his description of the poem as follows:

> Sir, knowing how doubtfully all Allegories may be construed, and this booke of mine, which I have entituled the Faery Queene, being a continued Allegory, or darke conceit, I have thought good . . . to discover unto you the general intention and meaning . . . I chose the historye of King Arthure, as most fitte for the excellency of his person, being made famous by many mens former workes, and also furthest from the daunger of envy, and suspition of present time. In which I have followed all the antique Poets historicall, first Homere, who in the Persons of Agamemnon and Ulysses hath ensampled a good governour and a vertuous man, the one in his Ilias, the other in his Odysseis: then Virgil, whose like intention was to doe in the person of Aeneas: after him Ariosto comprised them both in his Orlando: and lately Tasso dissevered them againe, and formed both parts in two persons, namely that part which they in Philosophy call Ethice, or vertues of a private man, coloured in his Rinaldo: the other named

Politice in his Godfredo. By ensample of which excellent Poets, labour to pourtraict in Arthure, before he was king, the image of a brave knight, perfected in the twelve private morall vertues. . . .

Spenser mentions four of his predecessors, Homer, Vergil Ariosto, and Tasso. (In the case of Homer it is a little unusual tha Spenser should choose Agamemnon rather than Achilles as the central figure of the *Iliad*, but Achilles sulking in his tent would make a poor comparison with the 'gentle knight' who begin Spenser's poem.) The two Italians are representative of an import ant tradition of writing which has not yet been discussed, the epic poetry of Spain and Italy. The tradition goes back at least to the twelfth century, to the great folk epics, the *chansons de geste*. These oral tales of war and chivalry, which have close relatives in the Icelandic Sagas and the Scandinavian Eddas (and of course the Anglo-Saxon *Beowulf*) were the work of the singers known in France as troubadours, or trouvères. One of the greatest of the *chansons* was the *Song of Roland*, composed in France around 1100 dealing with the defeat of part of Charlemagne's army at Ronce vaux. About fifty years later another historical figure, Roderigo Diaz, was the subject of the Spanish *Poema del Cid*, written almost within memory of the hero, who died in 1099. At the end of the same century the German hero Siegfried was celebrated in the *Nibelungenlied*, the most emotional and largest in scale of the three the direct ancestor of Wagner's operas. All three works have the single-minded drive of oral poetry, and they are heroic poems closer in spirit to the *Iliad* than the *Odyssey*.

If one is to compare these oral poems with Homer, their suc cessors in the sixteenth century, Ariosto, Camoens and Tasso stand in a similar relation to Vergil. Ariosto's poem, *Orlando Furioso* (1532) has the original Roland as its hero, but almost completely transformed. Between *The Song of Roland* and *Orlando Furioso* the French romances of chivalry and courtly love had intervened, assimilating the Arthurian legends and adapting them

to the newly defined codes of love and honour. In Italy, a genera-
tion before Ariosto, Boiardo had written a sprawling poem
Orlando Innamorato; Ariosto's work gives form and balance to the
earlier material. The poem is organized, like Dante's, into *cantos*;
these were originally a unit of length, the amount which an oral
poet could sing in one evening, but the term *canto* passed from the
Italian into the common language of epic, to be adopted by many
later writers (beginning with Spenser) as their standard sub-
division.

The poems of Camoens (*Os Lusiadas,* 1572) and Tasso (*Gerusalemme Liberata,* 1575) have been discussed at length by Sir
Maurice Bowra in *From Vergil to Milton;* Bowra shows how
Camoens attempted to rival Vergil, not simply in the line of his
poem, translated by Fanshawe as

> Arms and the men above the vulgar file,

but in the celebration of Portugal itself which the whole poem
achieves; the title, *Os Lusiadas, The Sons of Lusus,* even surpasses
that of the *Aeneid,* which refers only to a single man; Lusus is a
mythical eponymous hero of Lusitania. The hero of the poem is
Vasco da Gama, the great discoverer, and the work becomes a
poetic history of Portugal culminating in Gama's passage to India.

Tasso takes the concept of the Chivalrous Epic further even
than Camoens, for his poem, *Gerusalemme Liberata,* was closely
associated with the Crusades, and one of its heroes, Rinaldo, was
an ancestor of Alfonso II, Duke of Ferrara, for whom Tasso wrote
the poem; the work was intended to encourage a new Crusade to
the Holy Land. The poem often employs the supernatural and
magical for effect, and enchantment and allegory are intertwined;
but the castles, devils and haunted forests are only a part of this
Christian epic. As Bowra comments:

> Though in the *Gerusalemme* we may miss the humour and the

humanity of the *Orlando Furioso*, it is just because Tasso's poem is s
serious that it can claim to be a real epic and not a chivalrous romance
(*From Vergil to Milton*, p. 192

This is the background to Spenser's introductory letter to Raleigh
in 1589, fourteen years after Tasso's poem had been published; and
as Spenser was working on his *Faerie Queene*, a contemporary of
his was making a translation of the poem which was at Spenser'
elbow, Ariosto's *Orlando Furioso*. Sir John Harington's translation
came out in 1591, the result of an unconventional Royal Command
It appears that Harington, godson of Queen Elizabeth, had translated the risqué tale of Jocundo from Canto 28 of *Orlando* and
circulated it among the Queen's ladies in waiting. The Queen, in
real or pretended anger, banished him from Court until he had
translated all 40,000 lines of the poem. Ben Jonson announced
(predictably) that 'John Harington's Ariosto under all translation
was the worst', but in fact it has admirable life and pace, with a
rich vein of irony together with an accurate sense of the courtly
nature of the poem, so that the reader is often torn (as he is with
Chaucer's *Knight's Tale*) between admiration and laughter
Harington also was aware, no less than Spenser, of the allegorical
value of the poem, and included in his folio edition a 'Brief and
Summary Allegory' of the epic.

Characteristic of the translation as a whole is the first canto to be
translated, the twenty-eighth. Jocundo, who has been deceived by
his wife, visits the king of Padua, and discovers that the king is
deceived by his queen. After binding the king by oath not to take
revenge he tells him of both infidelities, and the two men resolve
to travel abroad to test the honour of women in general. At Jativa
in Spain they are both asleep with a girl who already has a lover, a
young Greek. At dead of night the Greek comes into the room:

> He takes a long and leisurable stride,
> And longest on the hinder foot he stayed;
> So soft he treads, although his steps were wide,

> As though to tread on eggs he were afraid;
> And as he goes, he gropes on either side
> To find the bed with hands abroad displayed;
> And having found the bottom of the bed,
> He creepeth in, and forward go'th his head.

The next morning Jocundo and the king tease each other about their sexual exploits, but each insists that he was asleep all night. Eventually the girl uncovers the truth:

> The king and his companion greatly mused
> When they had heard the practice so detected,
> And their conceits not little were confused
> To hear a hap so strange and unexpected;
> And though no two were ever so abused,
> Yet had they so all wrathfull mind rejected
> That down they lay and fell in such a laughter
> They could not see or speak an hour after.

The irreverence of the translator comes out strongly in the deliberte bathos at the end of each stanza, the tortuous syntax and rhyming. The effect is closer to Byron than to Spenser.

Spenser of course has his irony; but as he writes to Raleigh, 'The generall end therefore of all the booke is to fashion a gentleman or noble person in vertuous and gentle discipline.' The chivalry of the Arthurian legends and of the romances of Charlemagne become for him as important as the Crusaders' faith was to Tasso. The Faerie Queene, therefore, in this 'allegory, or darke conceit' is Gloriana, the Virgin Queen, Elizabeth, who 'beareth two persons, the one of most royall Queene or Empresse, the other of most vertuous and beautifull Lady', and each book has as its hero a knight associated with a particular virtue, the Red Cross Knight with Holiness, Sir Guyon with Temperance, and so forth. As the work develops Spenser draws into the poetry a great range of ideas and allusions from philosophy and literature, to give the poem a greater richness and inventiveness than any previous

English writer had achieved. This can be seen nowhere mo[...]
clearly than in the superlative twelfth canto of Book II, S[...]
Guyon's temptation at the Bower of Bliss, which owes so much [...]
the encounter of Odysseus with Circe in *Odyssey* 10 and Scyll[...]
Charybdis and the Sirens in *Odyssey* 12; but it has been full[...]
assimilated and allegorized into something as English as *Beowu[...]
It must be read aloud to be appreciated:

> On th'other side, they saw that perilous Rocke,
>   Threatning it selfe on them to ruinate,
>   On whose sharpe clifts the ribs of vessels broke,
>   And shivered ships, which had bene wrecked late,
>   Yet stuck, with carkasses exanimate
>   Of such, as having all their substance spent
>   In wanton joyes, and lustes intemperate,
>   Did afterwards make shipwracke violent,
> Both of their life, and fame for ever fowly blent.
>
> For they, this hight *The Rocke of* vile *Reproch*,
>   A daungerous and detestable place,
>   To which nor fish nor fowle did once approch,
>   But yelling Meawes, with Seagulles hoarse and bace,
>   And Cormoyrants, with birds of ravenous race,
>   Which still sate waiting on that wastfull clift,
>   For spoyle of wretches, whose unhappie cace,
>   After lost credite and consumed thrift,
> At last them driven hath to this despairefull drift.

(F.Q. II, 12, 7–8)

Sir Guyon passes the Rock and the Sirens, till he comes to th[...]
'fairre Witch' in the Bower of Bliss, who is presented as the Virgi[...]
Rose and described in a stanza translated directly from Tass[...]
(G.L. XVI, 15) which is as old as poetry itself:

> So passeth, in the passing of a day,
>   Of mortall life the leafe, the bud, the flowre,
>   Ne more doth flourish after first decay,
>   That earst was sought to decke both bed and bowre,

Of many a Ladie, and many a Paramowre:
Gather therefore the Rose, whilest yet is prime, ...
Whilest loving thou mayst loved be with equall crime.

(*F.Q.* II, 12, 75)

ut Sir Guyon resists the temptation and destroys the Bower of
iss in the stanza quoted at the start of this chapter.

The *Faerie Queene* was written when Marlowe and Shakespeare
ere producing their best work. Its best qualities are those of
lizabethan literature, exuberance and largeness of thought com-
ned with an astonishing lyricism and a capacity for schematiz-
ion and complex allegory. At its best it is equal to anything in the
riod; as an epic it is both the summit of the chivalric tradition of
e *chansons de geste* and the central point in an English tradition
hich began with *Beowulf* and is still alive.

ILTON, PARADISE LOST

very chapter in this book has been an examination of some major
evelopment in the epic form. Some of the innovations (especially
erhaps those of Ovid and Dante) are so far-reaching as to be
most redefinitions of the possibilities open to an epic writer. Yet
ie great innovators are not always the finest artists – Shakespeare
as, in one sense, a highly conventional writer – and Homer's
elebrated successor, Vergil, is a good example of a writer excelling
ithin a tradition. Milton, the author of the English *Aeneid,* is
iother.

Yet the very phrase 'author of the English *Aeneid*' begs an
nportant question. To what extent can *Paradise Lost* be called an
inglish *Aeneid*'? In its form, certainly, the poem looks back
irectly to Homer and Vergil. Originally written in ten books, the
iaterial was reorganized into twelve for the second edition of
574. The action begins as Horace suggested it should, *in medias*
s, with the war in Heaven already fought and the rebel angels in

Hell, so that the events of the war have to be narrated, in the be
Homeric manner, as a 'flashback' in Book VI. (Aristotle said of tl
Odyssey that it was 'all recollection'). The poem begins as it shoul
with an invocation, 'Sing, Heav'nly Muse', and it abounds with
wealth of similes and epic conventions. But the most curso:
second glance at the opening of the poem shows us that it is n
simply classical pastiche:

> Of Man's first disobedience, and the Fruit
> Of that Forbidden Tree . . .
> Sing, Heav'nly Muse, that on the secret top
> Of *Oreb*, or of *Sinai*, didst inspire
> That Shepherd, who first taught the chosen seed,
> In the beginning . . .
>
> (*Paradise Lost* I, 1–2, 6–

Those last three words hold the key; this is not Homer or Verg
transposed into English, but the word of God.

Milton was not the first to choose a Biblical subject for h
'Heroic Poem', as the epic was called in the seventeenth centur:
In 1656 Abraham Cowley, better known as a Metaphysical poe
published a *Davideis*, in twelve books ('not for the Tribes sak
but after the Pattern of our Master Vergil') on the principle th:
the life of David offered a better subject for epic than the classic
heroes. In a defence of his poem he complains:

> It is not without grief and indignation that I behold that *Divine Scien*
> *(Poesie)* employing all her inexhaustible riches of *Wit* and *Eloquen*
> either in the wicked and beggerly *Flattery* of great persons, or tl
> unmanly *Idolizing* of *Foolish Women*, or the wretched affectation (
> scurril *Laughter*, or at best on the confused, antiquated Dreams (
> senseless *Fables* and *Metamorphoses* . . . They are all but the *Col*
> *meats* of the *Antients*, new-heated, and new set forth.

And Cowley concludes his argument:

Does not the passage of *Moses* and the *Israelites* into the *Holy Land* yield incomparably more Poetical variety then the voyages of *Ulysses* or *Aeneas*?

The result of all this strong talk was a barren work in rhyming couplets of no poetic merit. As a parallel to Milton's treatment, here are some lines from Cowley's description of Hell:

> There is a place deep, wondrous deep below,
> Which genuine Night and Horrour does o'erflow;
> No bound controls th'unwearied space, but Hell
> Endless as those dire pains that in it dwell.
> Here no dear glimpse of the Sun's lovely face,
> Strikes through the Solid darkness of the place;
> No dawning Morn does her kind reds display;
> One slight weak beam would here be thought the Day.

There is a witty concentration here on the intriguing, rather than the horrific, aspects of Hell, which engages the reader's interest, but not his feelings. It needs only to be compared with four lines of Milton's description (*P.L.* I, 61–4):

> A Dungeon horrible, on all sides round
> As one great Furnace flam'd, yet from those flames
> No light, but rather darkness visible
> Serv'd only to discover sights of woe . . .

Milton's image is also 'metaphysical', but there is an ingredient which Cowley lacks, passion, an almost religious need to convince.

Paradise Lost is not only a Biblical epic, however. It is also a great psychological narrative, probing into the deepest of moral and spiritual questions. In a celebrated passage discussing good and evil in his *Areopagitica* Milton describes how

> our sage and serious poet Spenser (whom I dare be known to think a better teacher than Scotus or Aquinas), describing true temperance under the person of Guyon, brings him in with his palmer through the cave of Mammon, and the bower of earthly bliss, that he might see and know, and yet abstain.

Dante's *Divina Commedia* had been a poem of this kind, a moral and spiritual epic. Not long before Milton, John Donne had attempted, in his poem *The Progress of the Soul*, of which only one canto of fifty-two verses was completed, to write an epic of human soul. In the words of Ben Jonson's somewhat inaccurate account to his friend Drummond of Hawthornden, he began with

> the soule of that Aple which Eva pulled, and therafter made it the soule of a Bitch, then of a sheewolf & so of a woman. his general purpose was to have brought in all the bodies of the Hereticks from the soule of Caine & at last left it in the body of Calvin. of this he never wrotte but one sheet.

The poem deserves Jonson's irony for, as it stands, it appears to have no chance of becoming a successful venture, and it remains as an intriguing attempt at satiric mock-epic a century before its time. It also suffers (as an epic) from being in stanzaic form, and from having a number of heroes, two criticisms levelled also by Dryden against the *Faerie Queene*.

That Milton was well aware of his many predecessors, and of their significance, is clear in a number of passages. In one of these, a description of the ranks of fallen angels, we are reminded in quick succession of Homer, Statius, Malory, Boiardo, Ariosto, Tasso and the *Song of Roland*:

> For never since created man,
> Met such imbodied force, as nam'd with these
> Could merit more than that small infantry
> Warrd on by Cranes: though all the Giant brood
> Of *Phlegra* with th'Heroic Race were joind
> That fought at *Theb's* and *Ilium*, on each side
> Mixt with auxiliar Gods; and what resounds
> In Fable or Romance of *Uther's* Son
> Begirt with *Brittish* and *Armoric* Knights;
> And all who since, Baptiz'd or Infidel
> Jousted in *Aspramont* or *Montalban*,

> *Damasco,* or *Marocco,* or *Trebisond,*
> Or whom *Biserta* sent from *Afric* shore
> When *Charlemain* with all his Peerage fell
> By *Fontarabbia.*
>
> (I, 573–87)

The reference to Arthur (Uther's son) and Lancelot, the Armoric knight, acts as a reminder that Milton had originally intended his epic to have King Arthur as its hero. Arthur is of course the natural choice for the hero of a British epic; and had Milton been seriously determined to write the English *Aeneid* Arthur would no doubt have remained the hero. The Genesis story was to have been used for a drama, perhaps similar to *Samson Agonistes,* called *Adam Unparadis'd,* but as work went forward on the two, Milton must have decided that the Biblical story was the only possible theme for his epic. We can follow part of his reasoning in a famous passage at the start of Book IX:

> Since first this Subject for Heroic Song
> Pleas'd me long choosing, and beginning late;
> Not sedulous by Nature to indite
> Warrs, hitherto the only Argument
> Heroic deemd, chief maistrie to dissect
> With long and tedious havoc fabl'd Knights
> In Battels feignd; the better fortitude
> Of Patience and Heroic Martyrdom
> Unsung; or to describe Races and Games,
> Or tilting Furniture, emblazond Shields,
> Impreses quaint, Caparisons and Steeds;
> Bases and tinsel Trappings, gorgious Knights
> At Joust and Tournament; then marshald Feast
> Serv'd up in Hall with Sewers, and Seneschals;
> The skill of Artifice or Office mean,
> Not that which justly gives Heroic name
> To Person or to Poem. Mee of these
> Nor skilld nor studious, higher Argument
> Remains. . . .
>
> (IX, 25–43)

We can feel some regret that Milton chose not to continue with Arthur as a hero when we read passages such as this. Sir Thomas Malory had of course used the Arthurian legend for his vigorous *Morte D'Arthur*, part original and part translation. Yet even in his rejection of such material Milton shows such a vivid sense of the medieval that one feels he could well have elevated Malory's prose to epic heights; but it should be said that the full sweep of Milton's verse at its best would have transformed whatever subject he had chosen.

Surprisingly, however, Milton's style has been treated to the harshest criticism as well as the highest praise. One of his critics, T. S. Eliot, writing very much as a practising poet, saw his verse as a bad influence and a barrier to the development of eighteenth- and nineteenth-century poetry. This judgement was echoed by professional critics, among them F. R. Leavis and William Empson, but for the reader, once he has mastered the superficial difficulties of the somewhat Latinate syntax and vocabulary, the verse (especially when read aloud) conveys its meaning with great clarity. It should be remembered that for the blind Milton this was truly an oral poem, and it is surely intended for the ear. The quotation from Book IX already given is the clearest proof of this. It contains a sentence of seventeen lines, but the logic of the whole passage is never in doubt, and – more importantly – the significant words are invariably in positions of major stress, often standing as the first word in the line.

Milton's style may be seen as magnificent or reactionary perhaps according to taste; but a more teasing problem in *Paradise Lost* has been raised in every century since its publication, and that is the uneasy suspicion that the character of Satan is far greater than it should be, while Milton's God is both less just and less admirable than one would expect. The strongest statement of the position occurs in Blake's *The Marriage of Heaven and Hell* (1793):

The reason Milton wrote in fetters when he wrote of Angels & God, and at liberty when of Devils & Hell, is because he was a true Poet and of the Devil's party without knowing it.

This judgement has been very ably countered in our own time by C. S. Lewis and Douglas Bush, among others, who note that one does not have to be a villain to create magnificent villains, as Shakespeare does in Iago. A parallel problem, however, still remains: who is the hero of *Paradise Lost*?

The bluntest answer to this question was given by Addison in the *Spectator*, when he insisted that one should not look for a hero in the poem, but that if one must, then it is the Messiah. The answer has not been found satisfactory, since Satan, God and Adam are all equally central to the work. A more acceptable formula might be that *Paradise Lost* is an epic in the same sense as the Old Testament Pentateuch, with its series of heroes, Noah, Abraham, Moses. So Milton's poem begins with the focus on Satan in Hell; Satan journeys to Earth in Book III; during this book the Son offers himself to God as the Redeemer of Man, who must fall. Book IV introduces Adam and Eve in Paradise, where they are joined by Raphael, who describes (Books V–VIII) the war in Heaven and the Creation, ending with a warning against Satan. In Books IX and X Adam and Eve are tempted and fall, so bringing Sin and Death into the world. The final two books are given up to a description by the Archangel Michael of the history of the world leading to the promise of redemption. The epic ends with the expulsion of the two humans from Paradise.

It can be seen from this brief description how the focus shifts gradually through the poem from Satan through Man to the Messiah. Milton's play, *Samson Agonistes*, has a far greater concentration on the central character, but *Paradise Lost*, with its sustained narrative and overriding theme of Man's first disobedience, is the true epic.

Yet *Paradise Lost* is not still read because it is an epic, but for two qualities in which it excels. The first is an exact awareness of psychology which Vergil would have envied. A supreme example of the subtlety with which Milton conveys such details occurs in Book IX. Until the Fall, Adam and Eve had tended to address each other with elegant titles: 'My Author and Disposer', 'sole partner and sole part of all these joys'. After the Fall, the couple rise 'as from unrest', and we hear Adam's first words to his wife (l. 1067):

> O *Eve*, in evil hour . . .

Milton's other great quality is one for which he is not often praised, a capacity for visual description that is sometimes breath-taking. There is the account of Adam and Eve asleep on their first night in Paradise (IV, 771–3):

> These lulld by Nightingales imbracing slept,
> And on their naked limbs the flowrie roof
> Showrd Roses, which the Morn repaird,

while close by we see Satan

> Squat like a Toad, close at the ear of *Eve*.

It is this ability to fix in a single image the essential elements of a situation which makes the scenes so easily visualized – an amazing feat for a blind poet, especially since there are whole areas in the poem where Milton is careful not to be too precise over details of time and space. As a final example one must choose one of the six fine similes between lines 283 and 363 of Book I, the description of Satan's angels springing up:

> As when the potent Rod
> Of *Amrams* Son in *Egypts* evil day
> Wav'd round the Coast, up calld a pitchy cloud
> Of *Locusts*, warping on the Eastern Wind,
> That ore the Realm of impious *Pharaoh* hung
> Like Night, and darkend all the Land of *Nile*:
> So numberless were those bad Angels seen

Hovering on wing under the Cope of Hell
'Twixt upper, nether, and surrounding Fires.

(I, 338–46)

It is the single word 'warping', with its very exact meaning of a bird veering away in an air-current, or a boat tacking across the wind, which makes the image so powerful; the effect is strangely eerie. When a poet can combine, as Milton did, such command of the total form and structure of his work with a lyric poet's feeling for the single image, he can claim to have written a major poem. Certainly, after looking closely at the texture of *Paradise Lost* one quickly loses one's surprise to learn from Milton's daughter that one of her father's favourite books was Ovid's *Metamorphoses*.

MOCK–EPIC AND IMITATION: POPE TO TENNYSON

The Augustan poets of the late seventeenth and early eighteenth centuries adopted a strangely ambivalent attitude to the early epics. On the one hand there is their obvious admiration for the ancients, especially Homer and Vergil, which resulted in two major translations. On the other, none of the leading poets attempted an epic, and Pope's *Rape of the Lock* is rather a skilful burlesque.

In their translations Dryden and Pope ignored the excellent example of Milton, who had rejected Cowley's 'heroic couplets' as unfit for epic. Dryden's *Aeneid* and Pope's *Iliad* come to us in the metre of *Absalom and Achitophel*. The couplet is a fine medium for satire (it had served this purpose in the Greek epigrams and those of Catullus and Martial) but it tends to interrupt the flow of the epics, and gives them a sententious quality that is almost entirely foreign to them. There would be more justification for the couplet in translating Ovid or Lucan. Dryden, nevertheless, in the preface to his *Aeneid* makes this claim:

I have endeavoured to make Vergil speak such English as he would have spoken, if he had been born in England, and in this present age.

What makes this statement partly true is that Dryden, and Pope after him, made a translation which is a genuine poem in its own right, with a distinctive character and even a rather courtly nobility. Pope, coming to Homer, confesses that had Dryden translated him,

> I would no more have attempted Homer after him than Vergil: his version of whom (notwithstanding some human errors) is the most noble and spirited translation I know in any language.

Pope's version takes its cue from the enthusiastic opening words of the translator's Preface:

> Homer is universally allowed to have had the greatest invention of any writer whatever.

There are few translations of Homer which have the delicacy of touch and the appreciation of the variety of tone which we find in Pope's version. As Pope himself said:

> It is a great secret in writing, to know when to be plain, and when poetical and figurative.

Pope's preface mentions an important work by the French critic Le Bossu, *Traité du Poème Epique* (1675), a book which sees the purpose of the epic as social and didactic, and Pope's *Dunciad* and *The Rape of the Lock* were both written with a purpose. The *Dunciad* is a savage attack on many of Pope's contemporaries, an apocalyptic poem with an oppressive sense of doom:

> Lo! Thy dread empire, Chaos, is restored;
> Light dies before thy uncreating word:
> Thy hand, great Anarch! lets the curtain fall;
> And universal darkness buries all.

Pope's earlier and more mellow poem, *The Rape of the Lock*, is perhaps the more perfect creation. The occasion, an actual theft of a lock of hair, offered Pope the opportunity for some penetrating social satire, so wittily executed as to reconcile the parties at variance over the potential insult. Charming and light though the poem is, however, there is no doubt about the bite of the satire; here is the rape of the lock itself, from Canto III:

> The peer new spreads the glittering forfex wide,
> To inclose the lock; now joins it, to divide.
> Even then, before the fatal engine closed,
> A wretched sylph too fondly interposed;
> Fate urged the shears, and cut the sylph in twain,
> (But airy substance soon unites again)
> The meeting points the sacred hair dissever
> From the fair head, for ever, and for ever!
> Then flashed the living lightning from her eyes,
> And screams of horror rend the affrighted skies.
> Not louder shrieks to pitying heaven are cast,
> When husbands, or when lap-dogs breath their last;
> Or when rich China vessels fallen from high,
> In glittering dust and painted fragments lie!

The passage begins in epic formality (note that the books are called cantos) with Pope resolutely declining to call a pair of scissors by their own name. Instead, we see the 'forfex', the 'fatal engine' or the 'shears' slicing through the sylph, Pope's equivalent of the gods in Homer and Vergil; and as in Vergil, Fate is in the background prompting the fatal engine – a phrase better applied to the Wooden Horse than to Lord Petre's scissors. With the lady's reactions to the theft the tone changes. The first, splendidly dramatic, couplet

> Then flashed the living lightning from her eyes,
> And screams of horror rend the affrighted skies

prepares well for the famous triple simile which follows, with its sardonic progression in order of importance from husband to lap-dog to best china. It is bathos, but perfectly judged and timed, as are all the poem's details. The last canto, the Fifth, ends with a burlesqued battle on the Virgilian pattern, strongly reminiscent of the Hunt of the Calydonian Boar in Ovid's *Metamorphoses* 8:

> While through the press enraged Thalestris flies,
> And scatters death around from both her eyes,
> A beau and witling perished in the throng,
> One died in metaphor and one in song.

The final scene is the metamorphosis of the lock into a star, after the pattern of Julius Caesar in the Ovid, or, of the more direct ancestors, Callimachus's *Coma Berenices* and Catullus's Latin version of the same poem. *The Rape of the Lock* is not in fact Augustan at all, but Alexandrian. It is also the best thing of its kind in English; its only rival was published a century later, Byron's *Don Juan*.

The similarities between the two poems are almost all stylistic; Byron perfected in his poem a poised, witty style with the anti-climax as its main weapon:

> The pleasant scandal which arose next day,
>   The nine-days' wonder which was brought to light,
> And how Alfonso sued for a divorce,
> Were in the English newspapers, of course.
>
> (Canto I, stanza 188)

Byron, like Pope, has a precise sense of the strengths of epic, and where, therefore, it can be parodied. Pope had written an outrageous *Receit to make an Epick Poem* in 1713, which began:

For the Fable.
Take out of any old Poem, History-books, Romance, or Legend, (for instance *Geffrey of Monmouth* or *Don Belianis of Greece*) those Parts of Story which afford most Scope for long Descriptions ... Then take a Hero, whom you may chuse for the Sound of his Name, and put him into the midst of these Adventures: There let him *work*, for twelve Books;

For the Moral and Allegory. These you may Extract out of the Fable afterwards at your Leisure: Be sure you strain them sufficiently.

Byron shows a similar engaging flippancy, based on sound facts:

> My poem's epic, and is meant to be
>   Divided in twelve books; each book containing,
> With love, and war, a heavy gale at sea,
>   A list of ships, and captains, and kings reigning
> New characters; the episodes are three:
>   A panoramic view of hell's in training,
> After the style of Vergil and of Homer,
> So that my name of Epic's no misnomer.
>
> (Canto I, stanza 200)

Don Juan is also a wonderfully digressive work, a quality it shares with the *Odyssey* and the *Metamorphoses,* to say nothing of Ariosto. In a paper entitled 'Byron's *Don Juan*: Poem or Hold-all?' John D. Jump suggests that while the poem has a kind of unity, in the development of its hero as a result of his experiences and in the continual interest of the narrator's personality, it is the poem's very discursiveness which gives it its character:

> It remains, when all has been said, a somewhat casually assembled work. I do not say this to discredit it. On the contrary, I believe that our sense of its author's uninhibited exuberance and copiousness is an important part of our experience as we read.

It may be that what distinguishes an epic is the freedom of movement made possible by its size, the ability to tell one's tale in as much detail – and even in as unusual an order – as one pleases. It is certainly this aspect of the epic which has been used most enthusiastically by writers of our own century; but this is for a later chapter.

Don Juan is a long poem, above all, a poem of accumulating humour and charm, of sustained virtuosity. C. S. Lewis is said to have written at the end of his copy of the poem 'Never again!'; but there must be many readers who would agree with W. H. Auden:

Speaking for myself, I don't feel like reading it very often, but when I do, it is the only poem I want to read: no other will do.

The nineteenth century produced no other epic poem of an originality comparable with *Don Juan*; but the century saw the publication of some remarkable epic imitations. Keats wrote his *Hyperion* before *Don Juan* had been published, and his preparation for writing it was a thorough reading of Milton's *Paradise Lost*. To this he felt he must add a sound knowledge of Homer and Dante, and we know that he **also** studied the Elgin Marbles from the Parthenon with care. He wrote to his friend Benjamin Haydon, the artist (who was himself fond of epic subjects for his work) that his new poem had a 'more naked and Grecian manner'. He also, however, spoke of *Hyperion* as an 'abstract' poem, and the poet's great achievement is to have raised it above the concrete, visible world, into the mysterious world of the primitive gods:

> Deep in the shady darkness of a vale
> Far sunken from the healthy breath of morn,
> Far from the fiery noon, and eve's one star,
> Sat gray-haired Saturn, quiet as a stone,
> Still as the silence round about his lair;
> Forest on forest hung above his head
> Like cloud on cloud. No stir of air was there,
> Not so much life as on a summer's day
> Robs not one light seed from the feathered grass,
> But where the dead leaf fell, there did it rest.
> A stream went voiceless by, still deadened more
> By reason of his fallen divinity
> Spreading a shade: the Naiad 'mid her reeds
> Press'd her cold finger closer to her lips.

The emotional sympathy with the old fallen chthonic religion goes deeper than any copying of Milton and Homer; and when the poem's reworked version, *The Fall of Hyperion*, was given Cantos rather than Books, the allegiance to Dante is more spiritual than

mitative. *Hyperion,* written by Keats in anguish while his brother
Tom was dying, is a step forward from the great lyric poems, even
if in style and manner it looks backwards. The author was saying
no more than the truth when he wrote to his brother George, as he
reached the end of the first book of *Hyperion:* 'I think I shall be
among the English poets after my death.'

Later in the century Matthew Arnold, William Morris, Browning
and Tennyson all produced epic works. Arnold was a fine classical
scholar, and in his classic *Lectures on Translating Homer* (1861)
developed the theory of the Grand Style, requiring of any translation of Homer that it should be rapid, plain, direct and noble.
Sohrab and Rustum is all these. It is also famed for its similes – often
more Miltonic than Homeric – which give the work much of its
character:

> Like some rich hyacinth which by the scythe
> Of an unskilful gardener has been cut,
> Mowing the garden grass-plots near its bed,
> And lies, a fragrant tower of purple bloom,
> On the mown, dying grass – so Sohrab lay,
> Lovely in death, upon the common sand.

The poem is also very much a Victorian poem:

> For we are all, like swimmers in the sea,
> Poised on the top of a huge wave of fate,
> Which hangs uncertain to which side to fall.

The same fatalism can be seen in Arnold's other epic, *Balder Dead,*
in style the more Homeric poem, based on the Scandinavian myth
of Balder the blind god, and the attempt to rescue him from death.
The Norse legend seems not to have stimulated Arnold's imagination as greatly as the Persian. Soon after its publication, however,
by a strange irony, the versatile William Morris, an Icelandic and
Norse scholar, chose a subject from Greek mythology for his
seventeen-book epic, *The Life and Death of Jason* (1867), a poem

in rhyming couplets which reads like a pale conflation of Chaucer and Milton, possessing all the weaknesses of both and the strength of neither. Perhaps Morris should have attempted the *Balder* and Arnold the *Jason*.

Two poems remain to be considered, both major works, and both in a strange way failing to achieve perfection. Tennyson's *Idylls of the King* was composed over a period of nearly half a century, the first fragment, *Morte d'Arthur*, appearing in 1842 and the complete poem of twelve *Idylls* in 1885. The title, with its suggestion of Theocritus and Hellenistic pastoral poetry, is something of a false trail; the king of the second half of the title, Arthur, Milton's original choice of subject, is more of an epic hero, and there are moments in the *Idylls* when one feels that the true English epic, with Arthur as its rightful hero, is about to be achieved. Yet once more the subject seems to escape, as it has done again in our own day, in the writings of Charles Williams, who dealt with the Arthurian legend in his beautifully formed, but essentially minor poem, *Taliessin Through Logres*. Indeed, Tennyson seems to be aware of the uneasy relationship between his poem and its original model when he makes the bard introducing the *Morte d'Arthur* laugh the poem off:

> Why take the style of those heroic times?
> For nature brings not back the Mastodon,
> Nor we those times; and why should any man
> Remodel models rather than the life?
> And these twelve books of mine (to speak the truth)
> Were faint Homeric echoes, nothing worth,
> Mere chaff and draff, much better burnt. . . .
>
> (*The Epic*, 35–41)

Yet a poet of Tennyson's stature does not work so long to produce a poem of no consequence, and the poem rises often to its subject. Pope had suggested Geoffrey of Monmouth's History (which included Arthur) in his *Receit to make an Epick Poem*, and

Tennyson was also inspired by two English versions, Malory's *Morte D'Arthur* and Lady Charlotte Guest's translation of the *Mabinogion*. The result is a poem of twelve related episodes in the tale of Arthur and Round Table, held together by the character of Arthur and by the passing of the seasons through the poem, from the Spring wedding at its beginning to its wintry final book, *The Passing of Arthur*, ending in the hope of Arthur's journey to the

> island-valley of Avilion;
> Where falls not hail, or rain, or any snow,
> Nor ever wind blows loudly; but it lies
> Deep-meadow'd, happy, fair with orchard lawns
> And bowery hollows crown'd with summer sea,
> Where I will heal me of my grievous wound.

The lines are an imitation of Homer's description of Olympus (*Odyssey* 6, 42 ff.), but they express also the philosophical nature of the poem. As Hallam, Lord Tennyson wrote in his *Alfred, Lord Tennyson, A Memoir* (London, 1907):

> If epic unity is looked for in the *Idylls* we find it not in the wrath of an Achilles, nor in the wanderings of Ulysses, but in the unending war of humanity in all ages – the world-wide war of sense and soul . . .
>
> (Vol. ii, p. 130)

Browning's *The Ring and the Book* was published in 1868, but it is in one sense the most experimental and forward-looking of all the works discussed in this chapter. The story is taken from a book found by Browning at a Florence bookstall, *The Old Yellow Book*, the story of a sensational murder and trial in Rome in 1698. The twelve books of Browning's poem describe the finding of the book, and give an account of the murder in ten books, followed by a conclusion. What makes the central ten books unique is that they are a series of monologues spoken by central figures in the murder and subsequent trial, so that the poem has no plot, but is instead a series of reports of the same events, each slanted in its own way.

The work therefore anticipates many modern artistic movements, notably Cubism, and many of the basic trends in modern verse writing. The whole poem of over twenty-one thousand lines must be read for its full effect, but from the start it is clear that no writer was better qualified for the task than the author of *Childe Roland, My Last Duchess* and *Soliloquy of the Spanish Cloister*. The author gives some hint of his method at the close of the poem:

> Art may tell a truth
> Obliquely, do the thing shall breed the thought,
> Nor wrong the thought, missing the median word.
> So may you paint your picture, twice show truth,
> Beyond mere imagery on the wall.

The poem (as the quotation makes clear) is difficult, and the reader must read it as a philosophical and psychological narrative rather than a detective thriller. The main reason for its difficulty is the stress inherent in the writing of a revolutionary work. This is the price we pay for the *avant-garde*.

5
Forms of Modern Epic

Before coming to an assessment of twentieth-century epic writing we should again pause to define the term. The two initial definitions ('a work of art surpassing the dimensions of realism' and 'a poem including history') express clearly two aspects of the tradition which have been noted many times, the large scale of each work, and its all-inclusiveness. Almost every use of the word 'epic' in everyday speech has the first of these connotations. Soon after the 1970 Cup Final, which was still drawn after extra time, the Chairman of the Football Association commented:

> This was not a classic, it was an epic.

The word was used with the same meaning by John Whiting in an ironic exchange from his play *A Penny for a Song*:

Timothy: . . . The situation is roughly this: myself, versus one hundred and seventy-five thousand Frenchmen.
Hallam: An epic situation, no less.

It was in this sense, and not as a clearly defined critical term, that films like *Ben Hur*, *The Ten Commandments* and *Gone With the Wind* were called 'screen epics'. They were long and weighty; they had a cast of thousands; the term seemed natural. More recently, films have been made which show more appreciation of epic form. Bergman's *The Seventh Seal*, for example, uses the symbols of the returning crusader, Antonius Blok, and his friends the travelling players with very much the same lightness of tone as is used in the *Odyssey* with similar symbols; the style of narration is easy and

unhurried, episodic, apt to digress. The film at its best is perhaps
the inevitable development of epic form. Eisenstein had surely
realized this when he used Milton's description of the War in
Heaven as a shooting-script for the battle on the ice in *Alexander
Nevsky*.

For those who do not recognize the cinema as the twentieth-
century epic form, the novel is a natural choice. So many novels
are concerned, like the *Odyssey*, with the various adventures of a
closely observed hero that it is possible to think of almost every
major novel as an epic. Some novels, however, consciously echo
the form of previous epics, and a brief examination of some of these
may mark out the broad lines of a still growing tradition.

The first novels were often the work of established dramatists.
Cervantes wrote thirty plays before the publication of *Don
Quixote* in 1615. The work revels in the freedom which can belong
to a novel by contrast with the more closely structured drama, and
Cervantes allows the adventures of his engagingly unheroic hero
to cover an area at least as wide as did those of Odysseus. *Don
Quixote* is very different from a Homeric epic, however. The tones
vary far more widely, the humour is broader, the satire bites more
deeply.

Rather more than a century after this classic picaresque novel had
appeared in Spain, Henry Fielding, another (less successful)
dramatist, turned to novel-writing, and on this occasion Homer
appears to have been a direct influence on the form of the novels.
Joseph Andrews (1742) was written as a parody on Samuel
Richardson's *Pamela*, a novel constructed out of imaginary letters.
In lampooning Richardson's book Fielding was determined to
give his own a better defined form, and for parts of the book the
Odyssey was used as a model. The influence of Homer and Vergil
can be seen even more clearly in Fielding's masterpiece, *Tom Jones*
(1749), perhaps the height of the picaresque novel in English
where 'picaresque' can have both its original sense (a work dealing

with rogues) and its derived meaning of a loosely constructed narrative held together only by the 'Life and Adventures' of its hero. The epic antecedents of the passage immediately before the description of Sophia Western (IV, 2) are obvious:

> Hushed be every ruder breath. May the heathen ruler of the winds confine in iron chains the boisterous limbs of noisy Boreas, and the sharp-pointed nose of bitter-biting Eurus. Do thou, sweet Zephyrus, rising from thy fragrant bed, mount the western sky, and lead on those delicious gales, the charm of which call forth the lovely Flora from her chamber. . . .

This is burlesque; but, like Pope's *Rape of the Lock,* it is the work of a man who appreciates, and admires, the object of the parody.

If these works are 'epic' in the sense of being expansive, rambling works 'surpassing the dimensions of realism', the eighteenth century also produced a mad masterpiece which expresses, better than any other early novel, the other aspect of epic, that it 'includes history'. Laurence Sterne's *Tristram Shandy* includes so much that it hardly finds space for its hero. The opposite of the picaresque novel, which has the hero as its sole unifying factor, Sterne's work is based on the good Homeric principle of the digression.

The full title of the book, *The Life and Opinions of Tristram Shandy,* is the first of many false trails, for the birth of young Tristram occurs only after two hundred pages of the novel have already passed. These are filled with the most attractive discussions between Tristram's father and Uncle Toby, a compulsive amateur military strategist. The discursive tone of the novel can hardly be illustrated briefly, but the opening of Chapter XXXIII of Book Six, one of Sterne's frequent authorial interventions, gives some impression of the witty (and tantalizing) style. The reader, incidentally, will wait in vain for the complement of the first verb:

> I told the Christian reader – I say *Christian* – hoping he is one – and if he is not, I am sorry for it – and only beg he will consider the matter with himself, and not lay the blame entirely upon this book, –

I told him, Sir – for in good truth, when a man is telling a story in the strange way I do mine, he is obliged continually to be going back wards and forwards to keep all tight together in the reader's fancy - which, for my own part, if I did not take heed to do more than at first there is so much unfixed and equivocal matter starting up, with so many breaks and gaps in it, – and so little service do the stars afford which, nevertheless, I hang up in some of the darkest passages knowing that the world is apt to lose its way, with all the lights the sun itself at noon-day can give it – and now, you see, I am lost myself! –

Almost a century after the publication of *Tristram Shandy* an American novel appeared which rivals both *Tom Jones* and *Tristram Shandy*, a masterpiece both of sustained narrative and of the art of the digression. Herman Melville's *Moby Dick*, the famous story of the search for the great White Whale by the ship *Pequod* under the fanatical leadership of its mad Captain Ahab, combines all the resources available to the epic novelist. In its one hundred and thirty-five chapters Melville not only covers the story of the hunt of the monster and the eventual death of Ahab with the 'stricken whale' in a vivid and highly imaginative narrative style, but during the course of the tale manages to insert a whole series of chapters of more or less factual material supplying the background. The book begins with an Etymology of the word 'whale', and a list of appearances of whales in literature (supplied by a 'late consumptive usher to a grammar school' and a 'sub-sub-librarian' respectively!) and there follow chapters on Cetology, Ambergris, Of the Monstrous Pictures of Whales and The Whale as a Dish. We are given at the same time a graphic (and again scrupulously factual) account of life on a whaling-boat, with chapters headed Nantucket, The Quarter Deck, The Chart, The Lamp, The Quadrant and The Cabin. The reader feels that the work indeed 'includes history' while at the same time he is caught up in the sweep of the narrative itself.

Much of the book's strength comes from Melville's delicate use of many epic conventions, invocation and simile, in addition to the beautifully organized digressions. And above all there is the massive central figure of Ahab, in the traditional epic role of man against monster, Odysseus facing Scylla and Polyphemus, Beowulf battling with the Dragon. To accompany the heroic theme Melville developed a style so allusive and filled with metaphor that the book has been seen as a sustained allegory. Melville wrote in a letter to Mrs Hawthorne (with his characteristic gentle irony):

> I had some vague idea while writing it that the whole book was susceptible of an allegorical construction

but in the closing chapter of the story we are aware of no allegory, but only of a sense of mystery, where the book's 'careful disorderiness' (Melville's own phrase) reaches its climax in the last appearance of the great sea-beast:

> Suddenly the waters around them slowly swelled in broad circles;
> then quickly upheaved, as if sideways sliding from a submerged berg
> of ice, swifly rising to the surface. A low rumbling sound was heard;
> a subterraneous hum; and then all held their breaths; as bedraggled
> with trailing ropes, and harpoons, and lances, a vast form shot
> lengthwise, but obliquely from the sea. Shrouded in a thin drooping
> veil of mist, it hovered for a moment in the rainbowed air; and then
> fell swamping back into the deep.

This is the primitive, unexplained world of Grendel's lake, where poetry begins.

Soon after Melville, Dostoievsky and Tolstoy published their own epic works, notably *Crime and Punishment, War and Peace* and *Anna Karenina*. These are epics in that they each have a great central theme and hero, but only one of them, *War and Peace* (the least successful of the three), can be said to exist against a background of a whole civilization. Raskolnikov in *Crime and*

Punishment, and Anna and Levin in *Anna Karenina,* like Docto
Zhivago in Pasternak's novel, are psychological studies made on a
epic scale, rather than epic heroes. On the other hand, Schweik, i
Jaroslav Hašek's novel *The Good Soldier Schweik,* while lackin
the weight of the Russian heroes, has a universal quality whic
accounts for his adoption by the Czech people as their nationa
spokesman. He is the only picaresque hero whose life has con
tinued after the last page of his novel.

J. R. R. Tolkien's *Lord of the Rings* can be compared with th
novels of Thomas Mann in their conscious use of epic method
Tolkien's collection of novels, set in a world not far distant fron
that of the *Nibelungenlied* and Wagner, take the form of a massiv
journey and employ a host of characters, some heroic, some darke
and more monstrous. Mann sets his novels, more chillingly per
haps, in the world we know, and in *The Magic Mountain* was abl
to create an environment, the sanatorium, which he used as
symbol for the enclosed world of the human being. In *Docto
Faustus* he created also a superb hero, the composer Adria
Leverkuhn. Where the novel gains by comparison with Goethe'
Faust is in its inclusion of a complete segment of German society
as the headlong career of the genius Leverkuhn pursues the sam
disastrous downward path as the German nation moving toward
war.

A distinctly twentieth-century artistic form which shares
boundary with epic, Cubism, has had a predictable effect on man
of the major prose works, from Proust's massive autobiograph
A la Recherche du Temps Perdu onwards. The viewing of the sam
series of events from a number of angles, which is the essence o
Cubism, gives effective shape to Lawrence Durrell's *Alexandri
Quartet,* where the four novels share the same time-plane whil
exploring the reactions of different characters to a set of events
More recently, the novel *Z* by Vasilis Vassilikos, an account of th
investigation into the death of Gregory Lambrakis, a left-win

politician, at Salonica in 1963, uses a method remarkably similar to that of Browning's *The Ring and the Book*. The same kaleidoscopic effect is achieved also in *The Tin Drum* by Günter Grass, where the dwarf hero Oskar beats out his autobiography on a tin drum from his bed behind bars in an asylum. The autobiography covers the years up to and including the Second World War; the novel is a magnificent successor to Mann's *Doctor Faustus* and offers strong evidence for the continuity of the tradition.

The last novel to be considered is the supreme example of the digressive, kaleidoscopic method, James Joyce's *Ulysses*. It was written in Paris at the height of the Cubist movement, but its inspiration is the word-spinning city of Dublin, with its pubs full of latter-day oral bards. The plot of the novel is simple: it is the story of a single day in Dublin, the 16 June 1904, and the journey of a certain Leopold Bloom through a variety of adventures in the streets of the city until he returns to his wife in the early hours of the following morning. Bloom is a Jew (Joyce has here taken a hint from Victor Bérard's *Les Phéniciens et l'Odyssée,* a book he knew well) so that the story's hero is both Ulysses and the equally ancient figure of the Wandering Jew. The book's structure is modelled on the *Odyssey,* in a pattern of the subtlest and most intricate correspondences. Each of the eighteen episodes, beginning with Telemachus (Stephen Dedalus) and ending with Penelope (Molly Bloom) is provided with a corresponding Scene, Hour of the Day, Bodily Organ, Parallel in Art, Colour, Predominant Symbol, and Technic. The equivalents for scene six, therefore, Hades (*Odyssey* 11) are: The Graveyard; 11 a.m.; Heart; Religion; White, black; Caretaker; Incubism. This episode is perhaps the simplest route into the novel for a reader coming from the *Odyssey,* and the passage introducing the bodily organ of the heart gives a clear picture of the virtuoso style of the novelist. The passage begins with a remark setting off a train of thought in Bloom's mind:

> '*I am the resurrection and the life*. That touches a man's inmost heart
> 'It does,' Mr Bloom said.
> Your heart perhaps but what price the fellow in the six feet by tw
> with his toes to the daisies? No touching that. Seat of the affections
> Broken heart. A pump after all, pumping thousands of gallons o
> blood every day. One fine day it gets bunged up and there you are . .

And as Bloom muses on life and death he comes to think about th
Last Judgement, and then, with a single word Joyce transform
him into Odysseus at the start of his journey home:

> Get up! Last day! Then every fellow mousing around for his liver an
> his lights and the rest of his traps. Find damn all of himself tha
> morning. Pennyweight of powder is a skull. Twelve grammes on
> pennyweight. Troy measure.

Stuart Gilbert comments: 'The Epic glory reduced to a little dus
in a skull.'

The massive achievement of the book – its variety of style an
tone, the brilliantly apt allusions and above all the feeling that on
really has got the whole of Dublin into one day and one novel
cannot of course be conveyed by quotation. As an epic it is at th
same time more complex than Ovid or even Dante, and almost a
direct as the *Odyssey*. James Joyce said of the hero:

> He's a cultured, all-round man, Bloom is.

There could be no better description. *Ulysses* is one of the world'
most civilized books. It may even in time be regarded as th
greatest of all secondary epics.

EPIC THEATRE

The picaresque novel has an important parallel in one major fiel
of modern drama. The term 'epic theatre' appears to have bee
invented by the German Expressionist Erwin Piscator in the 1920'
and was adopted by his more famous disciple, Bertolt Brech

playwright, poet and director of the Berliner Ensemble from 1949 to 1956. Both Piscator and Brecht began their careers with the great showman of German theatre and cinema, Max Reinhardt, who developed his early interests in the intimate drama of night-clubs and cafés into a vast project, the 'Theatre of Five Thousand', where huge audiences were gathered together to watch spectacles of truly epic proportions. An example of this can be seen in his staging of *The Miracle,* a play by Karl Vollmoeller, for which the entire theatre was converted to represent a cathedral, with the intention of involving the audience both intimately and as part of a mass of spectators. Reinhardt was the innocent originator of a dramatic theory which was later exploited in the Nuremburg rallies of the 1930s, but Piscator and Brecht, moving away from Reinhardt's more naturalistic theatre, developed the theory along quite different lines.

Piscator was the originator of a programme for drama which has since been called 'documentary theatre'; he saw the stage as a plat-form from which an actor or dramatist could instruct and educate, as well as give pleasure. The intention was that an audience should react positively to the play being presented, should in fact be moved to act against injustice. It was on this foundation that Brecht built his theory of 'epic theatre'. In a famous table of com-parisons offered in his 'Notes to the Opera *Mahagonny*', Brecht lists the differences between Dramatic Theatre and Epic Theatre. The list begins with the purpose of Epic Theatre; while Dramatic Theatre 'provides the spectator with sensations', Epic Theatre forces him to take decisions'. The most revealing comparisons, however, are those related to form:

Dramatic Theatre	Epic Theatre
growth	montage
linear development	in curves
evolutionary determinism	jumps

(*Brecht on Theatre* tr. John Willett)

The word 'montage' will strike a familiar chord after a reading o Ulysses or the Alexandria Quartet; 'in curves' as opposed to 'linea development' perfectly describes Tristram Shandy. The elemen that Brecht is avoiding is that aspect of tragedy which Aristotl describes in his Poetics, the involvement of the audience throug pity and terror in an emotional trance of sympathy with th characters. In the first volume of this series, Tragedy, (Londor 1969), Clifford Leech sums up the difference in a sentence (p. 30)

> Where epic and tragedy essentially differ, apart from the fact o performance, is that in epic we have 'tragic moments' in a contex which is characterized by amplitude and variety rather than concen tration and crisis.

Mother Courage and her Children, written at the start of th Second World War, centres upon the reactions of a single stoica individual to the passage of war across her country. The characte is presented as a blend of humour and cynicism somewhat remi niscent of Schweik. Mother Courage loses her three children partl as a result of her determination to make a living out of war, yet he attitude to the war is often one of flippant irony:

> Who's defeated? The defeats and victories of the chaps at the to aren't always defeats and victories for the chaps at the bottom. Not a all. There've been cases where a defeat is a victory for the chaps at th bottom, it's only their honour that's lost, nothing serious.
> (Scene three, p. 29; tr. Eric Bentley

Another of Brecht's plays, an adaptation of Marlowe's Edwar II, offers a useful hint that he may not have been the first write of epic drama. The qualities that drew Brecht to Marlowe wer presumably that breadth of mind that has already been noted i Elizabethan writing and the spectacular nature of Marlowe's work in both senses – his plays are intensely visual and almost grandiose Certainly Tamburlaine and Faustus, with their succession of scene and clinically observed characters, obey many of the rules of Brechtian Epic Drama.

The title of Epic has also been claimed – and here perhaps even more surprisingly – for Marlowe's contemporary, Shakespeare. In a persuasive article in the *Yale Review* for Autumn 1969, 'The Henriad: Shakespeare's Major History Plays', Alvin Kernan argues that in describing the passage from Richard II to Henry V, from Middle Ages to Renaissance, Shakespeare was doing for England something comparable to Vergil's Roman Epic. Ezra Pound puts the same case in his inimitable style:

> The plays, especially the series of history plays, which form the true English EPOS, as distinct from the bastard Epic, the imitation, the constructed counterfeit.
>
> *(ABC of Reading, p. 59)*

Strong though the case for the Histories may be, Shakespeare's *Troilus and Cressida* contains in a single play most of the essential elements of epic. The subject of the work must of course have influenced the treatment, particularly since Shakespeare relies heavily on the seven books of Chapman's translation of the *Iliad* that had been published in 1597. The play, however, is far more episodic and stark than even Homer's narrative, and the final sequence of disjointed scenes refusing to be organized into conventional tragic cadences, gives the play a raw immediacy which makes *Troilus and Cressida* a unique experiment in Shakespeare's writing.

Between Shakespeare and Brecht two important experiments in epic drama had been made, Goethe's *Faust* and Hardy's *The Dynasts*. Both plays would be difficult to stage (Hardy announces firmly that his play is 'simply for mental performance') and both cover a large area. Goethe's play, one of the great Romantic works, covers the career of Faust in a series of sharply realized scenes of great variety; the prevailing theme is aspiration (Goethe was almost as much scientist as writer) and the Byronic *homunculus* created by the scientist Faust is almost a parody of one aspect of Romanticism as it attempts to scale the heights, only to be shattered.

In 1850 Matthew Arnold wrote, in his *Memorial Verses* to Wordsworth:

> Time may restore us in his course
> Goethe's sage mind and Byron's force;
> But where will Europe's latter hour
> Again find Wordsworth's healing power?

And indeed, with the death of the authors of *Faust, Don Juan* and *The Prelude* no writer of truly epic scope presented himself; the only epic drama written between *Faust* and Brecht's redefinition of the form came from a major novelist.

Hardy's *The Dynasts* (1903), called an 'Epic-drama' by its author, is very much a drama written by a novelist. It covers a considerable period (the Napoleonic Wars), in seven Acts, divided into one hundred and thirty-one scenes and employing over seventy-five speaking characters, not to mention the 'Phantom Intelligences', Spirits and Angels who have a similarity with the Chorus of a Greek tragedy. The scope is certainly too large for a novel (it is noticeable how selective Tolstoy's *War and Peace* is by comparison) and equally for a conventional drama. Perhaps it is best regarded as a kind of film-script completed nearly a decade before the establishment of D. W. Griffith as the first director of epic films.

The only other English playwright to have written what could be called Epic Drama is the modern dramatist strongly influenced by Brecht, John Arden. One of his most recent plays, *Armstrong's Last Goodnight,* deals with an incident in medieval Scottish history in an exhilarating combination of Chronicle and Morality Play. The structure is episodic and the tone urgent; but it is not a simple imitation of Brechtian method. Arden in fact engages our interest through the power of his presentation. Yet Lawrence Kitchen is right to point to a feature of the play which has caused difficulty to English audiences:

> Some of the criticism which *Armstrong* has met seems to come from inadequate sympathy with epic drama, and indeed from uncertainty as to what epic does. What epic can't do is to accommodate private, esoteric states of feeling or complex analysis of character. From Vergil to screen Westerns, the characters act out the *type* of a Roman, a barbarian, an outlaw or whatever. The generic terms gun-man or law-man are of crucial importance. In this play we ought to be think-ing of political man, clansman, and man of God.
>
> (*Drama in the Sixties* p. 88)

This is an entirely new definition of drama; but it is also an exciting new view of epic. It does not, however, stray as far from the historical truth of epic as might at first be supposed. The point is put with admirable clarity by Martin Esslin in *Brecht: a Choice of Evils* (p. 110). He points out that Brecht intended his audience to be permanently aware that they were in a theatre, that they were not watching real events happening in front of them:

> They are to sit back, relax, and reflect on the lessons to be learnt from those events of long ago, like the audience of the bards who sang of the deeds of heroes in the houses of Greek kings or Saxon earls, while the guests ate and drank. Hence the term *epic* theatre.

MODERN EPIC POETRY

The epic is not commonly thought to have survived to our own day, though various works have been suggested as the last true epic. In fact, the form is still very much alive, and in a state of con-tinual development. In the field of poetry, as has already been suggested, the characteristic twentieth-century form appears to be collage, a natural development of epic's all-inclusiveness and discursiveness. Since the collage is used to build up a picture of the artist's own environment, the great modern epics (Pound's *Cantos*, Eliot's *Waste Land*, William Carlos Williams's *Paterson*, David Jones's *Anathemata*) should better be described as detailed autobiographies.

An early autobiographical epic (begun even before *Don Juan*) is Wordsworth's *Prelude*. Taken together with *The Recluse* (of which a portion, *The Excursion*, was published in 1814) the two long poems constitute an impressive autobiography. Wordsworth himself took the matter a stage further in his Preface to *The Excursion:*

> The preparatory Poem is biographical, and conducts the history of the Author's mind to the point when he was emboldened to hope that his faculties were sufficiently matured for entering upon the arduous labour which he had proposed to himself; and the two Works have the same kind of relation to each other, if he may so express himself, as the Ante-chapel has to the body of a gothic Church. Continuing this allusion, he may be permitted to add, that his minor Pieces, which have been long before the Public, when they shall be properly arranged, will be found by the attentive Reader to have such connection with the main Work as may give them claim to be likened to the little Cells, Oratories, and sepulchral Recesses, ordinarily included in those Edifices.

By the same token, the thirteen-book *Prelude* (first version 1805, second version 1850) was entitled *The Growth of a Poet's Mind.* The idea that the whole body of a poet's work (or a major part of it) may be taken as constituting an autobiography is one which has had great currency recently. *The Prelude* is also, quite overtly, an epic. The Muse, or inspiration for the work, is introduced in the fifth line, as a 'welcome Friend'; he is Coleridge, to whom the poem is addressed. The poem thus has the character of a number of oral tales told to this friend, tales which describe to him in detail the speaker's poetic and spiritual development from the first dedi-

cation to poetry, through his undergraduate years at Cambridge to
his visit to France and hopes for the Revolution, through his later
disappointment and beyond. Two important themes run through
the poem, expressed in the heading of Book Eight: 'Love of Nature
leading to Love of Mankind.' *The Prelude* is a work in which both
these loves are drawn together, by contrast with *Don Juan*. Byron
was no less a lover of Freedom (he supported the Greek revolution)
but the satirist and the human being were often at variance, to the
detriment of his poetry. Yet Charles Williams, the author of the
Arthurian sequence *Taliessin through Logres*, says of Wordsworth's
other epic that

> Though the *Excursion* has nobler poetry in it than *Don Juan* has, yet
> *Don Juan* is a better poem and more homogeneous poetry than the
> *Excursion*. It would be a saint, a 'holy fool' of poetry, who would
> consent to keep the *Excursion* and lose *Don Juan*. And his sanctity
> and his folly would be equal.

In the same essay on Wordsworth (from *The English Poetic Mind*,
1932), however, Williams goes on to commend the poet's habit
of introducing solitary figures into his work. This, together with
the many fine similes in the *Prelude*, lends the poem the distinctive
character of an epic; and of all the solitary figures there is none
more isolated than the central figure of Wordsworth himself:

> I dipped my oars into the silent lake,
> And, as I rose upon the stroke, my boat
> Went heaving through the water like a swan;
> When, from behind that craggy steep till then
> The horizon's bound, a huge peak, black and huge,
> As if with voluntary power instinct
> Upreared its head. I struck and struck again,
> And growing still in stature the grim shape
> Towered up between me and the stars, and still,
> For so it seemed, with purpose of its own
> And measured motion like a living thing,

Strode after me. With trembling oars I turned,
And through the silent water stole my way
Back to the covert of the willow-tree;
There in her mooring-place I left my bark, —
And through the meadows homeward went, in grave
And serious mood; but after I had seen
That spectacle, for many days, my brain
Worked with a dim and undetermined sense
Of unknown modes of being; o'er my thoughts
There hung a darkness, call it solitude
Or blank desertion. No familiar shapes
Remained, no pleasant images of trees,
Of sea or sky, no colours of green fields;
But huge and mighty forms, that do not live
Like living men, moved slowly through the mind
By day, and were a trouble to my dreams.

(Book I, 374–400; 1850 version)

This vision at Patterdale, which is described in almost mystical terms, became one of a long series of deeply felt visual incidents through which Wordsworth built up his own mythology of experience. In this mythology the poet's mind grows and acts. The creation of the complete poem from this pattern of inter-related incidents is a labour of great imaginative skill, and it is during the organization of the work that the epic, rather than the autobiographical novel, is formed.

Ezra Pound's *Cantos* are at first sight less well organized. There must be many readers who have been discouraged by the apparent lack of planning, as well as by the poem's genuine difficulties. The first problem is the poem's range of reference, including the Greek and Latin classics, Chinese and Medieval Italian history, detailed legal and economic theory, and the autobiographical details of a poet who has lived in Mid-West and Eastern America, London, Paris and Italy for long periods. The poem also includes the full range of reading of an extremely well-read man, another fact which has alienated those readers who are reluctant to dig into the poem for its treasures. The *Cantos* are certainly never gratuitously difficult, and they always repay study.

There are only two books which are essential to the understanding of the *Cantos*: the *Odyssey* and Ovid's *Metamorphoses*. In a letter to his father written in 1927 Pound outlines the main scheme in musical terms:

> Rather like, or unlike subject and response and counter subject in fugue.
> A.A. live man goes down into world of Dead.
> C.B. The 'repeat in history'.
> B.C. The 'Magic moment' or moment of metamorphosis, bust through from quotidian into 'divine or permanent world'. Gods, etc.

The allusion is to *Odyssey* Book Eleven in the first place (Odysseus, like Aeneas and also Gilgamesh, having penetrated the Underworld); then there is its counterpart in history, whenever a historical character, Malatesta, Adams or Confucius, takes a similar step into the dark; and finally the theme is reversed as a counter subject, B.C., in the 'moment of metamorphosis' which occurs when the everyday world approximates to the 'divine or permanent world'. Another traveller through the Underworld was Dante, and Pound has indicated clearly the importance for him of the *Commedia* in his most revealing comment on the *Cantos*:

> For forty years I have schooled myself . . . to write an epic which begins 'In the Dark Forest,' crosses the Purgatory of human error, and ends in the light . . .

Making this journey with Pound are an assortment of great historical figures, the Italian Sigismundo Malatesta, the Chinese Confucius, the Englishman Sir Edward Coke, and many others. They are chosen as *personae* in Browning's sense, as characters through whom Pound can express his ideas. The comparison with *The Ring and the Book* does not need to be stressed; Browning is there at the beginning of Canto II; and the analogy with Words-worth's 'solitary figures' is also quite clear.

The *Cantos* open with a fine rendering of *Odyssey* 11, beginning characteristically with a conjunction:

> And then went down to the ship,
> Set keel to breakers, forth on the godly sea, and
> We set up mast and sail on that swart ship,
> Bore sheep aboard her, and our bodies also
> Heavy with weeping . . .

but the Second Canto takes us directly by a metamorphosis to another ship, the ship of Ovid's *Metamorphoses* 3, discussed in an earlier chapter. Here is part of Pound's version:

> Ship stock fast in sea-swirl,
> Ivy upon the oars, King Pentheus,
>   grapes with no seed but sea-foam,
> Ivy in scupper-hole.
> Aye, I, Acoetes, stood there,
>   and the god stood by me . . .
> Heavy vine on the oarshafts,
> And, out of nothing, a breathing,
>   hot breath on my ankles,
> Beasts like shadows in glass . . .

So the collage is built up, and fifteenth-century Italy exists side by side with Homer's Greece or the China of Confucius. The reader makes the necessary connections. Canto IX ends with Sigismundo Malatesta:

> 'and built a temple so full of pagan works'
>   i.e. Sigismund
> and in the style 'Past ruin'd Latium'
> The filagree hiding the gothic,
>   with a touch of rhetoric in the whole
> And the old sarcophagi,
>   such as lie, smothered in grass, by San Vitale.

The words could just as well describe one aspect of the *Cantos*. Another is their lyrical beauty, which can be present even when the most important themes are discussed. Here is Usury (Canto XLV):

> Usura rusteth the chisel
> It rusteth the craft and the craftsman
> It gnaweth the thread in the loom
> None learneth to weave gold in her pattern;
> Azure hath a canker by usura, cramoisi is unbroidered
> Emerald findeth no Memling . . .

And in one of the Chinese Cantos (LIII) there is a third style, total simplicity:

> Tching prayed on the mountain and
>   wrote MAKE IT NEW
> on his bath tub
>   Day by day make it new

Pound indeed 'makes it new'; this if anything, is the 'poem including history'. T. S. Eliot said of the *Cantos*:

> they are the only 'poem of some length' by any of my contemporaries that I can read with enjoyment and admiration.

Pound's epic ranges over most of the world's areas and cultures. Its author was too cosmopolitan to write the 'American epic', the poem dreamt of by Emerson:

> Yet America is a poem in our eyes; its ample geography dazzles the imagination, and it will not wait long for metres.

Walt Whitman attempted such a poem in his *Leaves of Grass*. In this century William Carlos Williams may well have achieved it. His poem *Paterson* has as its subject an American city, Paterson, New Jersey, below the Passaic Falls; but Paterson is also the name of a person, who resembles Williams himself. The Author's Note to the poem observes that 'a man in himself is a city', and the author has said that in structure the book

> follows the course of the Passaic River, whose life seemed more and more to resemble my own; the river above the Falls, the catastrophe of the Falls itself, the river below the Falls and the entrance at the end into the great sea.

The poem resembles Pound's in two things: it is a collage of autobiographical matter (letters, reminiscences, newspaper cuttings) and it rises periodically into poetry of the greatest beauty and clarity, among them this Renaissance picture, a tapestry, from Book Five:

> slippered flowers
> > crimson and white,
> > > balanced to hang
> on slender bracts, cups evenly arranged upon a stem,
> > foxglove, the eglantine
> > > or wild rose,
> pink as a lady's ear lobe when it shows
> > beneath the hair,
> > > campanella, blue and purple tufts
> small as forget-me-not among the leaves.

A brief collection of introductory notes to the poem contains in its third paragraph:

> A taking up of slack; a dispersal and a metamorphosis.

The second phrase, 'a dispersal and a metamorphosis' sums up the essential quality of the modern poetic epic. Williams states as his credo: 'No ideas but in things'; this is true, and the astonishing fact is that all things seem to be present in *Paterson*.

There are two comparable English poems. *Anathemata*, by David Jones, is a poem of the old Britons, the traditions of the Celts, 'and a great many concepts and motifs of Welsh and Romanic provenance . . . within a kind of Cockney setting.' The author's Preface begins with a quotation from Nennius, author of the *Historia Brittonum*, 'I have made a heap of all that I could find', and continues:

Part of my task has been to allow myself to be directed by motifs gathered together from such sources as have by accident been available to me and to make a work out of those mixed data.

A characteristic passage, illustrating the author's ability (which he shares with Pound and Williams) for associating the heroes of different cultures, opens section II, 'Middle-Sea and Lear-Sea'. The section begins with Hector and proceeds, through Roman surveyors, to Britain and Cornwall:

> Twelve hundred years
>   close on
> Since of the Seven grouped Shiners
>   one doused her light.
> Since Troy fired
>   since they dragged him widdershins
> without the wall . . .

And the section closes with a passage describing the 'whole argosy of mankind':

>   and
> THE BIRDS DECLARE IT
>   that wing white and low
> that also leeward go
>   go leeward to the tor-lands
> where the tin-veins maculate the fire-rocks.
> The birds
>   have a home
> in those rocks.

The poem is allusive and difficult, much in the same way as Pound's, but it shares the best qualities of the *Cantos* also. It is not such an ambitious work, but there is no other poem in English which probes so insistently at the roots of our earliest legends.

Eliot's *The Waste Land* would not be called an epic, but it has many features in common with the other poems discussed here. It employs a wide range of allusion, forming the echoes into a mosaic of sense where the reader will make his own connections. Fine though the poem is, however, it is too single-minded and enclosed a vision of society to contain the discursive variety of epic; it is a strange irony that Eliot, by his own admission the most 'classical' of all his contemporaries, should never have attempted the oldest form of all.

Two other countries must finally be mentioned. Yugoslavia, the only surviving home of oral epic, has produced two writers who continue the tradition. The first is Ivo Andrić, whose novel *Bosnian Story* (1945), set in the Napoleonic War, well justifies the citation accompanying the award of the Nobel Prize for 1961 (the year after the Frenchman Saint-John Perse, whose epic *Anabasis* was translated by T. S. Eliot):

> For the epic force with which he has traced themes and depicted destinies from his country's history.

The second is the poet Vasco Popa. Popa groups all his works into cycles, each cycle expressing a different aspect of his personality and of his relationship to the world, so that the whole poetic output justifies Wordsworth's dictum that the poet's collected poems constitute a form of autobiography. Introducing the Penguin collection of Popa's poems, Ted Hughes comments:

> In his latest collection, *Secondary Heaven* (1968) the total vision is vast and one understands why he has been called an epic poet.

The other country is Greece, where the modern poets are always aware of the length of their tradition. Four names must be mentioned. First, Kostis Palamas, whose *Twelve Lays of the Gipsy* chooses the traditional form to develop a bardic poem with a very strong national character. More recently, Odysseus Elytis wrote an ambitious poem, *Worthy It Is*, where the Biblical Creation is combined with a vision of the history of Greece; the poem has had wide currency through the brilliant musical setting of Theodorakis. The author of *Zorba the Greek*, Nikos Kazantzakis, is as well known in Greece for his *Odyssey*, a vast poem of twenty-four books and 33,333 lines, continuing the story of Odysseus (as did Dante and Tennyson) after his return home. The hero embarks on a further voyage, searching for the source of the Nile, and finally reaches the ultimate freedom of death. The work has the symbolic complexity of a novel, combined with a fine lyric gift. Ironically, its greatest fault is its closeness in form to the original, a snare avoided by Joyce in his *Ulysses*. Kazantzakis's poem remains a massive act of homage to Homer, rather than an original poem in its own right.

The word 'epic' will perhaps never quite be defined; we began with formal hexameter poems and end with collage. The element which all these works have in common is a kind of expansiveness, the ability to open up, however briefly, the whole landscape as far as the horizon in every direction. My last quotation is from a poem still unpublished in Greek, by Takis Sinopoulos. It is called *Deathfeast* and is a reworking, in a few hundred lines, of what may be the central moment of European epic, Odysseus calling up the ghosts in *Odyssey* 11. The poet describes how his friends who died in the Greek Civil War return to him:

> A wave of tears scorched me. What was I, years speaking with,
> Years alone reviving lost faces and through the window came
> glory shaded gold light, all around benches and tables and
> windows, mirrors to the underworld. And they came
> one after the other, dismounting,
> Porporas, Kontaxis, Markos, Gerasimos,
> thick hoar-frost the horses and the day swerving
> through the numb air . . .

The majestic, haunting figures converse together, and in this tiny canvas once again history is included. Epic is not a matter of length or size, but of weight:

> One by one the voices grew calm.
> One by one as they had come they left.
> For the last time I watched them, I called to them.
> On the ground the fire sank and through the window came
>
> How a single star makes the night sky navigable
>
> How in the empty church with so many flowers
> the unknown dead in his finery, the body anointed.

In these closing lines, with their subdued similes, the modern poet achieves the pathos of Odysseus greeting his dead companions, or Priam weeping with Achilles over the body of Hector. He reminds us of the essential humanity of Homer's poems; and without humanity it would be pointless to attempt an *Iliad*, a *Beowulf* or a *Divine Comedy*.

Select Bibliography

Three general books are of particular value: W. P. KER'S *Epic and Romance* (1908) is still the basis for any discussion of the two parallel forms. H. M. CHADWICK's *The Heroic Age* (Cambridge 1912) and SIR MAURICE BOWRA's *Heroic Poetry* (1952) are essential investigations into the period of the early epics.

THE EPIC BEFORE DANTE

The criticisms of Homer by ARISTOTLE (*Poetics*), 'LONGINUS' (*On the Sublime*) and HORACE (*Ars Poetica*), and of Vergil by SERVIUS are interesting as near-contemporary reactions. The first three works are conveniently brought together in a recent Penguin Classic, *Classical Literary Criticism*, translated by T. S. DORSCH (1965).

Modern studies of Homer have either been centred on problems of composition or pursued a literary critical line. W. J. WOODHOUSE, *Composition of Homer's Odyssey* (Oxford 1930) and RHYS CARPENTER, *Folk Tale, Fiction and Saga in the Homeric Epics* (Berkeley 1946) are interesting studies of the element of folktale in the poems. A. B. LORD's *The Singer of Tales* (Oxford 1960) conducts an illuminating analysis of Homer's technique through a comparison with the modern oral bards of Yugoslavia. GILBERT MURRAY, *The Rise of the Greek Epic* (4th edn. Oxford 1934) is an early work on the authorship problem; similar problems are dealt with by D. L. PAGE in *History and the Homeric Iliad* (Berkeley 1959) and *The Homeric Odyssey* (Oxford 1955), books which are as readable as they are erudite. Equally attractive is M. I. FINLEY's *The World of Odysseus* (1956), a fine guide to the social and economic background of the Homeric poems. Of the (far fewer) works of literary criticism, c. h. whitman's *Homer and the Heroic Tradition* (Cambridge, Mass. 1958) stands out. Finally, three books offer comprehensive studies of the relation of the background to the poems: a. j. b. wace and f. h. stubbings, *A Companion to Homer* (1962), g. s. kirk, *The Songs of Homer* (Cambridge 1962), abridged as *Homer and the Epic* (1962) and w. f. jackson knight, *Many-Minded Homer* (1968).

Among the most useful critical works on *Beowulf* are the early book by w. w. lawrence, *Beowulf and Epic Tradition* (Cambridge, Mass. 1928), *The Digressions in Beowulf* by a. bonjour (Oxford 1950) and dorothy whitelock's *The Audience of Beowulf* (Oxford 1951).

The Secondary epics have attracted a wealth of commentary. From the works on the Latin authors one might select w. f. jackson knight's *Roman Vergil* (revised and augmented 1966), the essay by t. s. eliot, 'What is a Classic?' in *On Poetry and Poets* (1957), brooks otis, *Vergil, A Study in Civilized Poetry* (Oxford 1963) and the admirable recent book by kenneth quinn, *Vergil's Aeneid, A Critical Description* (1968). l. p. wilkinson's *Ovid Recalled* (Cambridge 1955) includes a characteristically urbane study of the *Metamorphoses*.

DANTE AND HIS SUCCESSORS

The chapter on Dante (*Inferno* 10) in erich auerbach's *Mimesis* (tr. W. Trask, Princeton 1953) is excellent, as are the earlier chapters on the *Odyssey* and the *Song of Roland*. auerbach's *Dante, Poet of the Secular World* (Chicago 1961) is also important. t. s. eliot's essay, 'Dante' (1950) has recently been reprinted in paperback form.

From the immense volume of criticism on the Renaissance epics, sir maurice bowra's *From Vergil to Milton* (1945), which outlines clearly the tradition including Camoens and Tasso, is essential reading. GRAHAM HOUGH's *Preface to the Faerie Queene* (1962) and C. S. LEWIS's *A Preface to Paradise Lost* (1942) are both stimulating. IRENE SAMUEL, *Dante and Milton* (Cornell 1966) offers a detailed study of the influence on Milton of the *Commedia*. DOUGLAS BUSH, *Paradise Lost in our Time* (Oxford 1945) and A. J. A. WALDOCK, *Paradise Lost and its Critics* (Cambridge 1947) are two of the many fine books on Milton.

The following works have been found especially useful for the later epics: the Macmillan Casebook on *The Rape of the Lock*, edited by JOHN DIXON HUNT (1968), containing a wide range of contemporary and modern critical comments; ERNEST DE SELINCOURT's edition of the *Prelude* with 1805 and 1850 texts on facing pages (revised by HELEN DARBISHIRE, Oxford 1959); E. F. BOYD, *Byron's 'Don Juan': A Critical Study* (New Brunswick, N. J. 1945 and London 1958) and J. D. JUMP, *Byron's 'Don Juan': Poem or Hold-All?* (Swansea 1968); A. K. COOK's *Commentary on The Ring and the Book* (1920); W. D. ANDERSON, *Arnold and the Classical Tradition* (1965); STUART GILBERT, *James Joyce's Ulysses* (1930, revised 1952); HUGH KENNER, *The Poetry of Ezra Pound* (1951); MARTIN ESSLIN, *Brecht: A Choice of Evils* (1959).

Also valuable are the volumes in the 'Twentieth Century Views' series, General Editor MAYNARD MACK, on Homer, Vergil, *Beowulf*, Dante and Milton. Two issues of the magazine *Agenda*, edited by WILLIAM COOKSON, devoted to Ezra Pound (October/November 1965) and David Jones (Spring/Summer 1967) are especially stimulating.

TRANSLATIONS

Some fine modern translations should be mentioned: RICHMOND

LATTIMORE's *Iliad* (Chicago 1951) and *Odyssey* (New York 1967); ROBERT FITZGERALD's *Odyssey* (1961), less stately, but more a poem than Lattimore's. T. E. SHAW's *Odyssey* (1935) is the vigorous, intelligent version which one would expect from Lawrence of Arabia. EDWIN MORGAN has done a verse translation of *Beowulf* which suggests the poem's alliteration without artificiality (Berkeley 1952). More recently, KEVIN CROSSLEY-HOLLAND has produced an equally successful translation (1968). C. DAY LEWIS's verse *Aeneid* (1952) compares favourably with JACKSON KNIGHT's prose version (1956), but Homer has translated better to the twentieth century. ROBERT GRAVES is the author of a perverse, but illuminating version of the *Pharsalia* (1956) and W. S. MERWIN has made a sensitive translation of *The Poem of the Cid*, published with the original on facing pages (New York 1962).

All in all, the epic has probably never been better served by translators than in the past two decades.

Index